WHY NOT HER?

A MANIFESTO FOR CULTURE CHANGE.

LINDA COOGAN BYRNE

Why Not Her? Publishing © 2025

Copyright © 2025 by Why Not Her? & Linda Coogan Byrne

All rights reserved. No part of this publication may be reproduced, distributed, or transmitted in any form or by any means without prior written permission from the copyright holders.

The unauthorised scanning, uploading, or distribution of this book constitutes a theft of the author's intellectual property. If you wish to use material from this book (other than for review purposes), please obtain permission by contacting **Why Not Her?** through the **Contact Us** page at www.whynother.eu.

Thank you for supporting the author's rights.

Hardback ISBN: 9781036915872
Paperback ISBN: 9781036916213

For the girls.

CONTENTS

Preface vii
Introduction... xiii

Chapter 1: Amplifying Voices: Where the Journey Begins 1
Chapter 2: Beyond the Stage: Dismantling Systemic Inequalities... 11
Chapter 3: The Power of Data.. 21
Chapter 4: Turning Data Into Action 25
Chapter 5: The Boundless Potential of Women 35
Chapter 6: The Light Switch Moment......................................44
Chapter 7: Diving Into the Data 49
Chapter 8: Driving Change: The People and the Proof.............. 60
Chapter 9: Follow the Money and Amplify Your Influence 76
Chapter 10: Why Not Her? Turning Visibility into Victory....... 82
Chapter 11: Resilience and Renewal in a Post-Covid World 87
Chapter 12: We Don't Have the Budget... 93
Chapter 13: The Sound of Change 99

Epilogue: Looking Forward: The Movement Continues &
    An Activist's Toolkit for Change................................ 105
Afterword: The Fire That Keeps Us Moving............................. 113
References and further reading...115
Books & Articles... 117
100 Women in Music You Should Know (UK & Ireland)......... 119
About the Cover Artwork.. 121
About the Author 123
Sources & Attributions... 125

PREFACE

Culture change starts with a willingness to evaluate ourselves, our systems, and the underlying injustices that shape our world. This manifesto is more than a call to action—it's an invitation to reflect, a challenge to confront systemic bias, and a roadmap for meaningful, lasting change.

Here, I examine the gender inequities that define the music industry and stretch far beyond it. Through personal experience and data-driven analysis, I trace the patterns of exclusion that silence women and other marginalised voices. You'll read about their struggles, resilience, and hard-won victories. But this isn't just about exposing injustice—it's about accountability and tools for transformation.

This is a journey of resistance, resilience, and reform. Where you go from here—that's up to you.

To be completely open, I never considered myself a feminist. Not until I realised that the questions I asked, the resistance I encountered, and the battles I fought were, at their core, feminist acts. Education gave me the tools to navigate both my professional and personal life, but privilege alone didn't bring me here. My traumas shaped me into an activist. And in that space, I faced a fundamental question: how do we dismantle gender inequality?

The answer wasn't opinion—it was data. I believed for years that passion and persistence could drive change, that my voice alone could make an impact. But real progress only started when I collected and presented indisputable facts. That's when the doors began to creak open. That's when the shift started.

When I first looked up the definition of data, I found:

Facts and statistics collected for reference or analysis. Ironically, the example given was: *"There is very little data available."*

That struck a nerve. Across countless industries, data gaps continue to erase and exclude. For centuries, history has been written by the victors—while others were systematically omitted. My work began with asking, *Who is missing?* and demanding, *Why?*

For a long time, I believed we had made huge strides towards equality. I read about the suffragettes—Emmeline Pankhurst and the Women's Social and Political Union—who risked their lives fighting not just for the vote but for recognition in a world determined to silence them.

Their struggle is still ours. A century later, women are dismissed, mocked, and punished when we challenge the status quo. The battlegrounds may have shifted—from the streets to boardrooms, from courtrooms to digital spaces—but the resistance (you will hear this word *a lot* throughout this book) to our voices remains eerily familiar.

Women today are still labelled too emotional, too aggressive, too difficult. When we bring forward well-founded arguments, we're dismissed as erratic, while men making the same points are heralded as visionaries. I know this because I've lived it.

This book has been rewritten more times than I can count. Not just because of perfectionism, but because external forces have tried to erase it. The first completed draft, finished in 2021, was wiped from existence when hackers targeted my computer and servers. Before that, I was warned to "shut up and stay in my box." When I refused, I saw what *or else* truly meant: erased files, offline websites, vanished social media accounts, relentless attempts to destroy my credibility. The message was clear: stay silent.

The suffragettes were beaten, jailed, force-fed. Their suffering wasn't just to punish them—it was to send a message to every woman watching. *Stay in your place, or suffer the same fate.* The methods have changed, but the objective remains the same: intimidation and erasure.

I have watched people I trusted—those who once stood beside me—step back when the backlash became too great. Fear of losing status, of upsetting the patriarchy, of being targeted themselves. Their quiet retreat was a message in itself: *Don't burn bridges, Linda. Know your place.*

But what, exactly, is my place? Silence? Compliance? Accepting a system designed to suppress voices like mine? That may be comfortable for them, but it is not good for me. And it is not good for the women who come after me.

The suffragettes knew change is never convenient. Resistance always has a cost. But they fought anyway. And so will I.

Whether it's the 1900s or today, when women challenge inequality, we become a threat to a system that thrives on our suppression. This manifesto is my own act of defiance. A refusal to be silent. A commitment to continue carrying the torch, just as those before me did.

My entry into the music industry was the start of a journey I never expected—one that led me to fight battles not just against individuals, but institutions built to exclude. I was trained for this long before I arrived. I already knew what it meant to survive through chaos. I already knew what it meant to endure abuse. That history didn't just shape me—it gave me the strength to keep going.

Reading feminist thinkers like Mona Eltahawy, Ijeoma Oluo, and Caroline Criado Perez was like pouring petrol on a smouldering fire inside me—one I didn't even realise had been lit. They didn't just clarify my thoughts or validate my anger; they gave me purpose. And with that purpose came rage. The more I read, the more I researched, the more I saw the scale of injustice—and it swallowed me whole.

When I submitted an earlier version of this book to a publisher, an editor gave me blunt feedback: scattergun, chaotic, tangential. It stung—hard. But he was right (thank you, Ivan). His honesty forced me to step back, refine, and realign. I rewrote it because this message deserves clarity. This book isn't just a personal journey—it's a manifesto for change. This is for every survivor who was told to stay silent.

We should not have to navigate the world in fight or flight mode, gripping keys between our fingers, sharing our location, rehearsing escape routes. Our bodies are not invitations for harm. Our presence is not permission for violence. Yet we are the ones expected to modify our behaviour—to avoid certain streets, change our routines, shrink ourselves—while the real perpetrators walk free.

Safety is not a privilege. It is a right. And yet, the burden of avoiding harm always falls on us. This has to change. We must dismantle the systems that erase, steal, and suppress our voices.

If the truth makes people uncomfortable, so be it. Progress isn't about protecting sensitivities—it's about dismantling the structures that perpetuate harm.

For too long, history has been written by the powerful, at the expense of the silenced. It's time to rewrite it.

If you shine a light for others, you allow those in darkness to see possibilities they never imagined. If you amplify a voice, you make space for others to be heard.

This book is dedicated to those who are unafraid to ask difficult questions, no matter the consequences.

And finally, remember this: you are here because your mother, and her mother before her, survived a world that was never built for them to thrive in. That world is changing. And so are we.

Open your mouth.
Raise your voice.
Sing your song.
Tell your story.

We rise when we stand together—with truth and the courage to speak up. Change begins the moment we refuse to be silent.

— Linda

INTRODUCTION

This manifesto is a call to action. A demand for change. A reluctance to accept the mechanisms that have kept women and marginalised voices out of the spotlight for far too long, particularly in the music industry.

This book is not just about recognising problems. It's all about accountability. It is about eliminating the systems that maintain the existing quo and offering the resources to construct something better. It is about tackling the unseen barriers that prevent people from reaching their full potential in an industry still dominated by antiquated norms.

I will guide you through these concerns, using personal experiences, stories of perseverance, and hard-hitting research to expose the disparities we can no longer ignore. Together, we will investigate, critique, and rewrite the narratives that have created the business, envisioning a future in which equality is a reality rather than an unattainable goal.

This manifesto will take you on a journey through:

- ✓ The Root of the Problem – We begin by exposing the historical and cultural forces that have shaped today's inequities.

The structures that were never designed to include us. The doors that were built to remain closed.

- ✓ The Voices of Resistance – Through personal stories and lived experiences, we honour the women and marginalised voices who have fought—and continue to fight—against an industry that too often tries to erase them.
- ✓ Redefining the Future – Most importantly, we will look forward. How do we break the cycle? How do we create a culture where inclusion is the norm, not the exception?

This is more than a manifesto. It's a movement.

It's an invitation to those who are ready to stand up, to listen, and to be part of a change that will leave a lasting impact.

The question is—are you ready?

Chapter 1

AMPLIFYING VOICES: WHERE THE JOURNEY BEGINS

"Ní Saoirse go Saoirse na mBan: There is no freedom until the freedom of women."

–Old Irish Proverb

Life can seem extremely complex, and how we manage it is influenced by elements such as gender, ethnicity, and privilege. The music industry offers a particularly vivid lens through which to explore these inequalities. It's a space where success is not just about raw talent—it's about who gets the platform to showcase that talent. The stories of whose voices are amplified and whose are sidelined reveal far more than individual ambition; they shine a spotlight on deep-seated structural biases that shape society at large. Whatever your birthplace or cultural background, one thing is certain: the playing field is not level and sadly, it never was. For instance, if you are a white male, the path to success is oftentimes smoother with fewer obstacles and greater chances of access to opportunities for recognition.

A prime example of this can be seen and indeed heard in the music industry. Success in any area requires more than simply skill or diligence; it also requires opportunities, and doors being opened for us to grow, be nourished and be able to flourish. It's about conquering challenges, speaking up, and becoming known as the protagonist of your own story. It involves crafting a song that so captivates listeners that it seemingly floats to the top of the charts on its own.

For Irish and British male artists, personal struggle has often been a cornerstone of their rise to fame. Artists and male fronted bands like Dermot Kennedy, Ed Sheeran, George Ezra, Coldplay, Snow Patrol, Hozier, and The Script have written anthems rooted in resilience and hardship—songs that have dominated the charts. Their music is raw, emotional, and deeply relatable. Audiences embrace their stories, welcoming their pain as a shared, universal experience without question. Pure acceptance. Their voices and their stories matter.

Think about Hozier's "Take Me to Church," Dermot Kennedy's "Outnumbered," or Coldplay's "Fix You." Their songs voice genuine hardships that people can relate to, giving them widespread radio play, public devotion, and critical recognition. Their music is not only heard, but celebrated, demonstrating that vulnerability, when conveyed by specific voices, can result in global success.

The truth is, the reception these artists receive reflects a much bigger dynamic. Their talent is undeniable—I mean, I'm a diehard Dermot Kennedy fan. I even flew to Holland to see him live because his Irish tour was sold out! But their success isn't just about talent. It's about operating in an industry—and a world—that amplifies certain voices while others are left fighting to be heard. Their achievements shine not only because of their skill but also because of the privileges and structures that allow some voices to thrive with far fewer obstacles.

This is not intended to diminish their accomplishments; rather, it is to acknowledge the unequal foundations upon which success is constructed. The first step toward true change is to address these disparities and create an industry in which every story has an equal chance of being heard, regardless of who tells it.

What about the women?

Most Irish female artists' experiences are vastly different. The team and I in the Why Not Her? collective conducted a 20-year analysis of the Irish Singles Chart, and the results lay it bare:

- For every female act that reaches the chart, 4.6 male acts do the same.
- Male acts have seven entries for every single entry by a female act.
- For each week a female act spends on the chart, a male act spends 11.5 weeks.
- 71.1% of top 10 singles over the past two decades were released by Irish male artists and bands.

Here is a visual to show you just how dismal it is when it's laid out like this. Looking at this contrast should make it clear just how deep the imbalance runs.

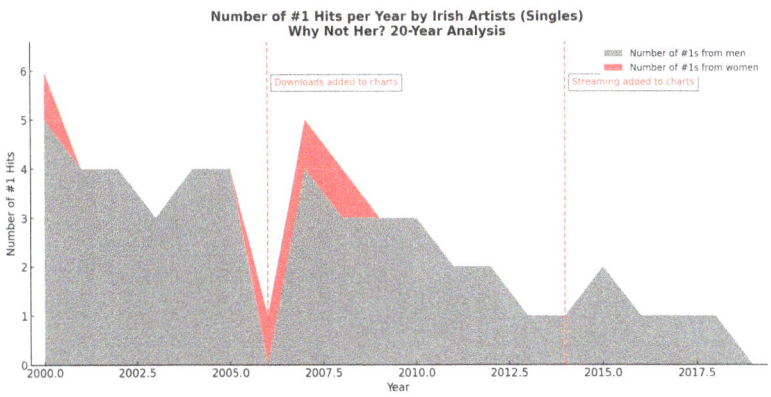

The scale of exclusion is staggering. Women, and especially women of colour, have been absent from mainstream success. Between 2010 and 2020, not a single Irish woman reached the top rank.

Then came Irish Women in Harmony—47 women joining forces to record a powerful rendition of "Dreams" by The Cranberries. Their voices didn't just break a decade-long drought; they raised vital funds for Safe Ireland, supporting women and children experiencing domestic abuse.

The single went on to reach Number 15 on the Official Irish Singles Chart and Number 1 on the Official Irish Homegrown Chart—a chart dedicated to highlighting the most popular songs by Irish artists across streaming, downloads, and sales. This feat marked the first time a female act topped the Homegrown Chart and the first time in over a decade that an Irish female act had broken into the Top 20 of the Official Irish Singles Chart.

It took nearly 50 women coming together to reclaim a space that male artists often occupy alone. Even imagining that contrast should tell you everything.

Needless to say, the system isn't broken—it was built this way. And it's long past time to change it.

This isn't a coincidence. It's a pattern. Male artists dominate radio playlists and festival stages, leaving women to fight for scraps—or feeling isolated if they are among the tiny percentage of female headliners. And airplay, which is the lifeblood of chart success, is gate-keeping in a way that excludes them. Even when women write about resilience, adversity, and triumph, their voices don't get the same platform or visibility.

Let's take a look at Festival slots

Then we look at the live scene… Festivals are more than just celebrations of music; they're critical platforms where careers are made or broken. They represent the ultimate validation—an artist's ticket to larger audiences, bigger opportunities, and greater industry backing.

Yet, the gender disparity in festival lineups mirrors the same systemic barriers that women face across the entire industry. The imbalance is not just disappointing; it's a glaring reflection of how talent is nurtured, rewarded, and sustained. Let's take a closer look at how festivals are faring in their responsibility to represent women.

The figures from 2024's major UK and Irish festivals reflect both progress and ongoing obstacles in achieving gender equality in music. But first, let's take a quick look at where things currently stand.

Glastonbury 2024 (UK): Two of the three Pyramid Stage headliners were female: Dua Lipa and SZA, alongside Coldplay as the sole male headliner. This was a notable step forward, but zooming out, only around 25% of the total lineup featured female musicians or female-fronted bands (Book More Women, 2024). While having two female headliners is progress, the overall roster remained heavily male-dominated, proving that festival gender balance is still a work in progress.

In 2023, Glastonbury co-organiser Emily Eavis addressed the issue, stating, *"We're doing our best, but the pipeline is simply not there."* She pointed to efforts to nurture female talent by offering more opportunities on smaller stages, aiming to build a stronger pool of future headliners. The intention is clear—at least they're trying, which is more than can be said for many festivals.

Looking ahead to 2025, there's already speculation about a more varied and inclusive lineup. Media reports suggest that artists like Olivia Rodrigo, Charli XCX, Sabrina Carpenter, Chappell Roan, Raye, Lola Young, and Doechii could be part of next year's roster. If there was ever a time to actually book more women, it's now.

Other Festivals in 2024

The gender disparity at Glastonbury is reflective of a larger trend seen across major festivals:

Reading & Leeds 2024 (UK): 18% of the lineup featured female artists or female-fronted bands (Book More Women, 2024). Out of six headliner slots, only one was filled by a solo female artist (Lana Del Ray). While RAYE performed, she was not a headliner. In 2021, after backlash over its 91% male lineup, organiser Melvin Benn remarked, "We book the acts that are available." However, little progress has been made, as the 2024 lineup remained overwhelmingly male.

Electric Picnic 2024 (Ireland): Disappointingly, less than 20% of the Electric Picnic 2024 roster featured female musicians or female-led ensembles. While Kylie Minogue was one of the festival's few female headliners, the rest of top-billing positions were taken by male musicians such as Calvin Harris, Noah Kahan, Gerry Cinnamon, and Kodaline.

Year after year, critics have pointed out the chronic gender gap at Electric Picnic. Despite increased awareness and pressure on festivals to enhance representation, female performers are still disproportionately underrepresented.

This isn't just about appearances; it's about opportunity. Festivals serve as a key venue for launching talents, increasing visibility, and establishing future headliners. If women are not allowed equal representation on these stages, they are systematically excluded from industry advancement.

Latitude 2024 (UK): The festival made some strides in gender representation, with 42.36% of the lineup featuring female artists or female-fronted acts (A2D2, 2024). However, headliners still skewed male. London Grammar, fronted by Hannah Reid, was the only female co-headliner, performing alongside Duran Duran, Keane, and Kasabian. While this is an improvement, it still falls short of full gender parity.

Longitude 2024 (Ireland): Contrary to previous years, female artists were present in the headliner slots, with Becky Hill and Doja Cat among the festival's leading names. While this marks some progress, overall representation across the lineup still lagged behind.

Longitude 2025 (Ireland): And then… we're back to square one. The festival's initial lineup announcement sparked criticism for its extreme gender imbalance. Out of 19 performers, only one—DJ Hannah Laing—is female, bringing female representation to a pitiful 5.26% (District Magazine, 2024). Sure, more acts might be announced later, but this pattern is impossible to ignore. And I am sure Hannah isn't too happy to be the only female act on the lineup.

Reading and Leeds 2025 (UK): Finally, some good news—Chappell Roan has been announced as a headliner alongside Hozier and Travis Scott. Roan's inclusion is a much-needed win for female representation on major festival stages, proving that progress, though painfully slow, is possible when the industry actually makes the effort.

Across these major festivals, the same pattern emerges: Women make up less than a quarter of most festival lineups. Male artists still dominate headliner slots. Even festivals that claim to be working toward gender balance continue to fall short.

It's 2025. How is equality in festival lineups still such an uphill battle? Here's a clue: it's all connected to a broader systemic issue.

Who Decides Who the "Biggest Acts" Are?

Festival organisers love to dismiss criticism with the same tired excuse: *"We just book the biggest acts."* But that falls apart when you ask the obvious question—who decides who the biggest acts are?

Success in music isn't a coincidence; it's a carefully cultivated cycle built on visibility. And who controls that visibility? Radio airplay. Streaming algorithms. Industry-backed campaigns. It's a system, and it overwhelmingly favours men.

For an artist to reach "main act" status, they need the right platforms. Radio fuels chart success. Streaming algorithms push certain names to the top. Festivals amplify exposure, drawing in new fans and industry buzz. Male artists dominate these opportunities, building followings, racking up sales, and becoming the "safe bets" organisers book year after year. Meanwhile, women and gender-diverse artists—locked out of these career-defining spaces—are left fighting tooth and nail to prove their worth. Without the same access, how can they ever break through to become the "biggest acts" festivals claim to prioritise?

Take Lizzo, for example. Before *"Truth Hurts"* became a global anthem, she spent years grinding, pouring everything into her music with little recognition. Even after reaching stardom, she's still not spared from the industry's double standards. Instead of being celebrated solely for her incredible talent and creativity, she's constantly up against the male gaze: *Is she too fat? Too loud? Too much?* Questions male artists never have to face. Men get to perform, exist, and succeed without being dissected or told to shrink themselves into some arbitrary mould.

Similarly, CMAT, the Irish singer-songwriter, faced a wave of body-shaming after her performance at BBC Radio 1's Big Weekend in 2024. The abuse was so severe that the BBC disabled comments on the performance video. CMAT responded by shutting down the noise with facts, stating:

"By the way, I am an award-winning songwriter that has released two albums which were received to 'universal acclaim'."

Here's the truth: artists like Lizzo and CMAT already work ten times harder just to get a seat at the table. And even when they break through, they're still saddled with double standards and scrutiny that their male counterparts never encounter.

So when organisers say, *"We just book the biggest acts,"* without acknowledging how rigged the system is, it's a weak excuse. Success isn't neutral when the deck is stacked. Until the industry removes these biases and creates equal pathways for everyone, the *"biggest acts"* defence is nothing more than a way to maintain the status quo.

This isn't just a representation issue—it's a blockade. The industry doesn't just reflect demand; it creates it. Festival organisers, booking agents, and labels decide whose names are in bold on posters, whose music reaches the biggest crowds, and whose careers flourish. When those choices overwhelmingly favour men, the industry isn't passively biased—it's actively reinforcing inequity.

This isn't about pitting men against women. Inclusion doesn't take away from male artists; it expands opportunities for everyone. Festivals thrive when they showcase variety—fresh perspectives, new sounds, and a lineup that reflects the real world.

A world where women make up 50% of the population shouldn't have festival bills where they're a token presence. Music was never meant to be a closed loop for a select few—it's meant to evolve, reflect diversity, and welcome all voices. Ending gatekeeping is the first step to achieving that.

These glaring disparities in festival lineups mirror the systemic obstacles that women and marginalised voices face in every corner of society, from boardrooms to classrooms to political offices.

I always say that the inequities in the music industry are a symptom of something much larger—deep-seated systemic structures that dictate who succeeds, who suffers, and whose stories are told. After all, everything is connected.

The music industry is a microcosm of the world at large. Bold statement? Maybe. But stay with me. It mirrors the same patterns of inclusion and exclusion, visibility and invisibility that play out across workplaces, politics, education, and every corner of society. When we dissect these dynamics in music, we uncover a blueprint for systemic inequity—one that stretches far beyond the festival stage or the radio playlist.

In the next chapter, we'll dive deeper into how these disparities are woven into the fabric of society and, more importantly, explore actionable ways to start unravelling them. Because if we can decode inequity here, in an industry as universal as music, then we have a roadmap for creating change everywhere.

Chapter 2

BEYOND THE STAGE: DISMANTLING SYSTEMIC INEQUALITIES

"The systemic change we need isn't about tearing anyone down—it's about building everyone up."
—Roxane Gay

The gender disparities evident in festival lineups (and on radio and streaming playlists - which we will look at in the next few chapters) are more than isolated industry phenomena—they are symptomatic of deeper, systemic inequities that ripple across all facets of society. Festivals, as public spaces of cultural expression, provide a striking lens through which we can explore these issues. While the music industry serves as the primary focus of this manifesto, it also acts as a microcosm of much broader societal structures that dictate who gets opportunities, whose stories are heard, and who is left behind.

By stepping back from the music industry, we can see how these patriarchal frameworks not only shape creative spaces but also influence how we define success, handle adversity, and allocate value in our lives.

The music industry is but one thread in a much larger tapestry. The inequities we observe there—from who gets booked at festivals to whose voices dominate airwaves—mirror the structures that dictate opportunities in every other sphere of life. These patriarchal frameworks seep into education systems, workplaces, and even our homes, shaping not just who succeeds but how we perceive success itself. To truly understand systemic inequality, we must broaden our perspective beyond the stage and playlists.

These structures don't just dictate opportunities or gatekeep success—they shape everything from career progression to mental health, impacting men, women, and gender-diverse individuals alike. The pressure for men to adhere to outdated notions of masculinity is as damaging as the systemic silencing of women's voices. This conditioning runs deep, with consequences that are undeniably severe, particularly regarding mental health, as evidenced by the harrowing realities of suicide.

Mental Health and the Impact of Patriarchy

OECD (Organisation for Economic Co-operation and Development) data highlights a troubling reality: suicide rates are significantly higher for men than for women, with the methods often reflecting societal expectations shaped by patriarchal norms:

- Men gravitate toward hanging—violent and absolute, reflecting a societal expectation of stoicism and "strength."
- Women more often choose overdose—quieter and less confrontational, echoing a world that conditions them to avoid causing disruption, even in their final moments.

These patterns reveal how patriarchy harms everyone. Men are discouraged from showing vulnerability, taught to repress pain, and pressured to equate silence with strength, leading to high rates of suicide, burnout, and emotional isolation. Meanwhile, women's struggles are dismissed, their voices silenced, and their suffering neglected until it's too late.

Patriarchal norms perpetuate inequity and intensify economic inequality. Wealth hoarded by a privileged few, predominantly white men, creates ripple effects: women face fewer resources to escape toxic environments or access mental health support, while men are burdened with the pressure to "provide," often leading to despair and exhaustion. Breaking these barriers isn't just about redistributing wealth—it's about creating avenues for opportunity, dignity, and collective well-being.

The consequences of systematic inequity are evident. When a society prioritises the perspectives and experiences of one group over others, a toxic hierarchy emerges, silencing creativity, variety, and development. For males, the cost of rigid masculinity is emotional isolation, fatigue, and greater rates of mental health problems. For women and other groups, the cost is even higher—erasure, disdain, and an ongoing uphill battle for recognition and rights.

However, the cost to society as a whole is perhaps the most tragic: stifled innovation, decreased well-being, and a collective loss of opportunity. Equality is more than just a moral requirement; it is required for a healthy, balanced world.

Calling it as it is; toxic masculinity limits men as much as it oppresses women, perpetuating a culture that equates strength with silence and emotion with weakness. Its effects are devastating—shaping everything from mental health crises to societal inequalities. Addressing these concerns is more than just correcting a faulty system for one group; it is about developing a balanced, equitable society for all. True solutions must go beyond mere acknowledgment;

they must dismantle the deep-rooted inequalities that fuel harm and division across every level of our communities.

The Music Industry as a Microcosm

The music industry is a microcosm of these broader dynamics. Take the grim gender disparities in festival lineups as an example: male artists consistently dominate headline slots, while women and non-binary artists fight for visibility in supporting roles. This pattern mirrors societal inequalities in industries far beyond music. The systematic marginalisation of certain voices not only silences diverse perspectives but perpetuates a narrow and outdated view of who deserves success. These dynamics aren't confined to the stage—they echo through boardrooms, political offices, and classrooms, reinforcing a culture where privilege dictates opportunity.

- **Men's struggles** are amplified, celebrated, and rewarded.
- **Women's struggles?** They're lucky if they're even heard.

In Ireland, for instance, it took nearly 50 women collaborating to break a decade-long absence of Irish women at number one—a telling reminder of the systemic hurdles female artists face in gaining recognition. This moment wasn't just overdue; it was a glaring illustration of the structural barriers that persist in the industry. It's time to amplify every voice. This isn't just about music; it's about championing fairness, inclusion, and equality across all sectors.

Yes, I hear the argument that change is uncomfortable for men. After all, it challenges centuries of dominance where men held the reins as breadwinners and decision-makers. But let's ask this: have men, in their pursuit of success and stability, paused to consider the toll that systemic inequality takes on everyone else? Change may be difficult, but it's not impossible. It's essential.

Barriers for Women

When we dig into the numbers, it becomes impossible to ignore just how many more hurdles women must clear compared to white men. The system disadvantages women, and statistics prove it. Let's take a glimpse at wealth inequality and economic disparities.

The Racial Wealth Gap

The racial wealth gap didn't appear overnight. It directly results from policies that locked people of colour out of economic security. Redlining was an infamous practice in which banks and financial organisations denied minority populations loans, mortgages, and financial services, marking predominantly black or non-white neighbourhoods as "undesirable."

The effects of redlining linger, with:

- Property values in previously redlined areas remaining lower.
- Minority families having fewer assets to pass down.
- The wealth gap widening over generations.

The Gender Wealth Gap

- **United States**: For every dollar of wealth a single man owns, a single woman owns just 82 cents (NWLC, 2023).
- **United Kingdom**: Women hold just 40% of total household wealth, despite making up more than half the population (LSE, 2023).
- **Ireland**: Lone parents, 90% of whom are women, have a poverty rate of 41% (CSO, 2023).

The Impact on Children

- **Poverty rates for single-mother households:**
    - 1 in 3 children in single-mother households in the US lives in poverty.
    - In Ireland, 41% of lone-parent households face poverty.

- **Growing up in poverty leads to:**
    - Worse health outcomes.
    - Lower-quality education.
    - Fewer opportunities for upward mobility.

Wealth inequality hurts everyone. This isn't just about personal wealth. When a small, privileged group hoards wealth—especially white men—it hurts society as a whole.

Key consequences include:

- **Economic stagnation**: Keeping money in the hands of a few instead of circulating it in the wider economy slows growth.
- **Reduced social mobility**: Traps people in poverty and prevents them from climbing the economic ladder.
- **Undermined democracy**: Concentrated wealth gives the ultra-wealthy disproportionate control over policies and decision-making.

Who suffers the most in all of this?

- **Children**: Poverty means worse health, unstable housing, and limited access to education.

- **Single mothers**: Face higher rates of food insecurity and fewer opportunities to escape poverty.

Despite the daunting statistics, progress is being made in leadership across the UK and Ireland. Women are assuming more powerful roles, offering hope for systemic change. These women are more than just leaders; they are trailblazers, paving the way for others to follow. Their presence in positions of authority defies centuries-old standards, giving young girls real evidence that they, too, can lead.

However, this improvement should not lead to complacency. Representation is an important first step, but it must be followed by structural reforms that remove the impediments that continue to hold countless others back. True equality does not come from having a few exceptional women at the top; it comes from building a system in which every woman has the opportunity to advance.

I will never forget a tapestry of Mary Robinson, Ireland's first female President, that stood in the window of a shop I passed regularly on the bus into Dublin City. It was displayed in a standing frame for what felt like years, and every time I saw it, I was struck by the enormity of what it represented. Wow, she is the PRESIDENT!—a woman leading a nation, a symbol of change in a country where, for so long, power had been held almost exclusively by men.

Robinson herself famously said, "The hand that rocks the cradle can rock the system." It was a reminder to women everywhere—not just to take part, but to shake things up, to challenge, to lead. And to all the mothers out there reading this book, remember her words. The impact of your actions, your voice, and your presence in the world extends far beyond what society might have conditioned you to believe.

I mention some powerhouse women in politics below, but wouldn't it be wonderful to have more than just a handful of women to bullet point?

Ireland:

- Ivana Bacik (Labour Party leader): A distinguished barrister and academic with a personable leadership style.
- Holly Cairns (Social Democrats leader): The youngest leader of a political party in Ireland, with a background in sustainable agriculture.
- Mary Lou McDonald (Sinn Féin leader): A pivotal figure in Irish politics with a strong academic and political foundation.
- Michelle O'Neill (First Minister of Northern Ireland): Marking a significant step forward for female leadership in the region.

United Kingdom:

- Penny Mordaunt: Leader of the House of Commons and a key figure in British politics.
- Angela Rayner: Deputy Leader of the Labour Party and a prominent voice for equality.
- Kemi Badenoch: Focused on entrepreneurship and economic growth, bringing essential diversity to leadership discussions.

Having more women in leadership roles proves that change is possible. However, there is much work to be done:

- Ireland's parliament has the lowest percentage of female representation in Western Europe, at just 25%.
- Achieving 50% representation should be a collective goal. Collaboration is key.

The Reality of Harassment and Discrimination in Politics

It's great to see more women venturing into the domain of political leadership in the UK and Ireland—I'm here for it. They are my heroes because let's be honest, it's not all standing ovations and victory parades. More like a slow clap followed by a barrage of nonsense they shouldn't have to deal with. What's the reality? They're still navigating through a muck of discrimination, online abuse, and sexual harassment—apparently, some individuals can't handle women's thoughts and authority.

In 2018, a thorough investigation conducted by the Inter-Parliamentary Union (IPU) found that 6.2% of female MPs reported having been sexually assaulted and 24.7% had been sexually harassed during their time in office. Sadly, male coworkers from both their own parties and opposition groupings were responsible for 75.9% of these crimes. These occurrences frequently took place during election campaigns, political gatherings, and parliamentary buildings.

In Ireland, the situation is equally concerning. A study highlighted that women who contested elections reported experiencing political violence more frequently than their male counterparts. This included degrading talk, the spread of false rumours, and instances of political violence with sexual connotations. Such experiences not only harm the individuals involved but also pose challenges to efforts aimed at improving gender equality in political representation.

These difficulties are so widespread that they have far-reaching consequences. According to research published by the European Parliament Research Service in 2024, many incidences of violence against women in politics go unreported, with 46.7% of physical violence cases and 76.5% of sexual harassment cases not officially registered. Underreporting is frequently motivated by fear of punishment, societal stigma, or a lack of trust in existing support structures.

These difficulties highlight the urgent need for systemic transformation. Tackling the root causes of harassment and discrimination head-on, developing effective reporting and support systems, as in actually putting them in place and not just talking in circles around it, as well as cultivating a culture of respect and equality, are all necessary steps toward ensuring that women may participate fully, freely, and safely in democratic processes.

By confronting these issues head-on, we can work towards a political environment where the presence of women in leadership roles is not only celebrated but also protected and sustained.

Chapter 3

THE POWER OF DATA

"Data is a precious thing and will last longer than the systems themselves."
— Tim Berners-Lee

Data surrounds us every day, whether we realise it or not. It's in the songs we stream, the news we consume, and our choices as consumers. The rise of data has highlighted its importance—not just in understanding the world, but in using it effectively to bring about meaningful change. The inequalities discussed in the previous chapters painted a vivid picture of systemic imbalance. But how do we move from recognising the problem to actively dismantling it? This is where data became my weapon of choice. It wasn't just about identifying patterns; it was about proving what had long been felt but often ignored—disparities that were no longer anecdotal but irrefutable.

As a music consultant, I relied on data to inform clients about when, where, and to whom their music was being played. For years, I subscribed to Radiomonitor, a platform that tracks airplay and provides detailed analytics. Initially, I saw it as just a tool to achieve better outcomes for artists. Radiomonitor first appeared to be a convenience—a means to track airplay and plan better promotions. But during lockdown, as I spent hours reading through the numerous data points, I realised something profound: this wasn't simply a business tool; it was a window into the inner workings of an inequitable industry. The numbers were more than simply figures; they were stories ready to be told. Every statistic reflected who was being boosted and, more significantly, who was being overlooked.

I began to see data not just as numbers but as a tool to expose systemic inequities and demand accountability. Data, in its raw form, can appear cold and distant. However, when linked to personal experiences, it becomes something more. Each percentage point, each name absent from a playlist signified real people—artists who had dedicated their lives to their profession only to be silenced by a system that deemed them unfit. It was more than just exposing these disparities; it was also about giving a voice to individuals who had previously been silenced.

This is where the art of data storytelling became clear to me. Numbers alone can be overlooked, but when they are paired with lived experiences and human impact, they become undeniable. As I explored patterns, the disparities were glaring: women and marginalised artists were being excluded—not by accident, but by design.

For years, these inequities were hidden in plain sight. Radio stations' playlists and airplay decisions were shaped by unconscious biases, favouring familiarity and excluding diversity. These decisions weren't just about what was marketable; they were reflections of systemic inequities embedded within the industry. It was clear that the data I had at my fingertips could be the key to sparking meaningful change.

Digging Into the Numbers

As I dug deeper, patterns emerged that were impossible to ignore. Women and marginalised artists weren't just underrepresented; they were systematically excluded. The data revealed a grim reality: men, particularly white men, monopolised radio playlists to a degree that could no longer be brushed off as mere coincidence. Entire hours of programming passed without a single female or marginalised voice. This wasn't just about audience demand—it was a calculated pattern. And patterns, once uncovered, demand scrutiny. Who was making these decisions? Why were certain voices being consistently excluded? And, most importantly, who stood to benefit from this imbalance?

The deeper we dug, the clearer it became: this wasn't just an issue of taste; it was about power and profit. The artists who dominated the airwaves were often tied to the same booking agencies and record labels holding a monopoly over the industry. Airplay wasn't just exposure—it was a launchpad, a direct pathway to headlining festivals and filling arenas. And the system seemed to ensure these opportunities went to a select few.

The connections were impossible to ignore. DJs championing these "rising stars" on air were frequently seen uploading VIP footage from festival stages or backstage at high-profile concerts, mingling with the very label executives whose rosters they so enthusiastically promoted. The cosy relationship between radio, labels, and event organisers painted a troubling picture. It wasn't just about music; it was about maintaining a network of influence, with the same players benefitting from a system designed to uplift their own.

In some cases, male artists had five, six, even seven of their songs featured in the Top 20 most-played tracks on a single station. The repetition wasn't just excessive—it was suffocating. The data wasn't just a collection of numbers; it was a spotlight, revealing a system where the airwaves weren't just biased—they were leveraged, orchestrated, and, ultimately, bought and sold. While these connections might not breach legal boundaries, they raised serious questions about fairness, transparency, and the integrity of the entire ecosystem. How ethical is it all?

The next time you are in your car or listening to the radio somewhere, count the amount of male voices you hear in between the random anomaly of a female voice.

This wasn't just about playlists; it was about mindsets. The teams behind these radio stations often lacked diversity, leading to unconscious biases that perpetuated inequality. Analysing the data allowed me to pinpoint these gaps and prioritise the most pressing issues in my reports. It became clear that presenting this information compellingly was just as important as uncovering it. The true power of data lay in its ability to strip away excuses and force accountability.

The beauty of data is its ability to transcend opinion. It doesn't argue; it declares. By presenting these findings in an undeniable format, I could no longer allow gatekeepers to hide behind excuses. Whether it was a lack of awareness or deliberate exclusion, the numbers laid everything bare. And with this evidence in hand, I felt a responsibility—not just to present the truth but to demand change.

During those quiet lockdown months, I realised my role wasn't just to collect data but to use it as a megaphone—to influence conversations, dismantle complacency, and push for real action. This wasn't just about fixing radio playlists or festival lineups; it was about reshaping an entire industry. The stories hidden in those spreadsheets were bigger than music—they were a reflection of society's broader failures. And if I could use this data to start a conversation here, perhaps it could spark change elsewhere too. After all, inequity isn't confined to one sector; it's woven into the fabric of everything we do.

Chapter 4

TURNING DATA INTO ACTION

> "Data has the power to expose inequality and drive accountability. But it is not enough to see the numbers—we must act to transform them into justice."
>
> — Dr. Mary Robinson

Data is powerful because it removes ambiguity. It cuts through opinion and bias, offering an unvarnished truth. When I delved deeper into Radiomonitor's statistics, the patterns became impossible to ignore. Women and marginalised artists were excluded, their music receiving little to no airplay. This was not a coincidence—it was systemic. (That fecking word again!).

The reports that were created by myself and my team in Why Not Her? using this data weren't just about pointing out problems—they were about igniting action. At first, the numbers felt overwhelming, and honestly I couldn't believe what I was seeing in front of my eyes. The numbers felt like a flood of harsh truths I couldn't ignore. As I delved deeper, I realised their power lay not just in exposing disparities but in compelling change. Each statistic and chart felt like the wail of a banshee coming off the pages I was looking at, sounding off in my brain, a haunting cry echoing the systemic inequities that had been ignored for far too long.

For those unfamiliar, the banshee is a spectral woman from Irish folklore, a foreteller of fate whose unearthly cry signals an inevitable loss. She isn't the bringer of death but the messenger, her keening a warning that something is coming—whether people want to hear it or not. And therein lies the connection.

For generations, Irish women's voices, much like the banshee's, have been dismissed, feared, or outright silenced. The warnings they sounded—about inequality, about exclusion, about the cultural erasure they were experiencing—were waved away as exaggeration, just as the banshee's cries were once shrugged off as superstition. But the truth always reveals itself. The banshee's lament wasn't a myth; it was a reckoning. And so too were these reports.

In some myths, the banshee isn't just a signal of doom but a figure of mourning, keening for the loss that has already happened. In that way, she mirrors the women in this industry—forced to carry the weight of exclusion, their warnings dismissed, their voices trailing into the wind until, finally, someone listens.

I remember poring over the data late at night, seeing the reality of what was happening to women in Irish music laid bare in cold, hard numbers. The eerie thing was, we already knew this. Women in the industry had been crying out about it for years—just like the banshee, their voices trailing through the air, only to be met with denial, discomfort, or outright refusal to listen.

There's a long tradition in Ireland of women being seen as too emotional, too dramatic, too much. The banshee herself is feared not because she causes harm, but because she forces people to confront something they don't want to face. And isn't that exactly what happens when women speak uncomfortable truths? They are called difficult, disruptive, hysterical—anything but right.

But here's the thing about a banshee's cry: you can't un-hear it. Once she keens, the message is out in the world, and nothing can take it back. These reports were our own banshee's wail—undeniable, impossible to ignore, and signalling that a long-overdue reckoning was at hand.

Yet, during those early stages, even I doubted the sheer scale of the dismal findings and sought a fresh perspective.

I reached out to my friend, Áine Tyrrell, a folk artist who had relocated to Australia. Late into the night, Áine and I poured over the data, both of us stunned by the patterns emerging. Áine's insights were invaluable—not only because of her keen eye but also due to her personal experience. She had left Ireland, frustrated by the lack of support for Irish women in music, to build a successful career abroad. Now, she headlines festivals and receives the radio play and respect she was denied at home.

Áine once shared during a press interview, "I carry on the great Irish tradition of making art cradling that balance of joy and sorrow, pain and triumph. That's Irish as fuck."

Her words encapsulate the resilience and passion that many Irish female artists embody, yet often find unrecognised in their homeland. This phenomenon of talented women emigrating to pursue success elsewhere is all too common, reflecting a systemic issue that demands attention.

From Numbers to Narratives: The Role of Record Labels

One of the most significant discoveries was the relationship between airplay, visibility, and professional success. Artists who dominated the Top 20 playlists reaped the rewards: commercial opportunities, profitable tours, and industry backing. Yet, those excluded from these coveted charts, no matter their talent, remained invisible. Their potential was stifled by a system that prioritised what it deemed "marketable."

This question again: who chooses what is marketable? Part of the answer lay with those who historically held the power: record labels. Their decisions shaped the soundtracks of nations, reinforcing a cycle of exclusion and invisibility for others.

A poignant example is the experience of British singer-songwriter Raye. Signed to Polydor Records in 2014 under a four-album contract, she faced significant barriers in releasing her music. Despite her dedication—working tirelessly and adapting her style to meet the label's constant demands—Raye was prevented from releasing a full album. In June 2021, she voiced her frustration on social media, stating:

"I have been on a 4 ALBUM RECORD DEAL since 2014!!! And haven't been allowed to put out one album. ALL I CARE ABOUT is the music." (x.com)

This situation took a toll on her mental health, leading to anxiety and bitterness. She shared:

"It would dictate my mood, my anxiety." (theguardian.com)

Raye's experience highlights the profound impact record labels have in determining an artist's marketability and the challenges artists face when their creative visions don't align with corporate expectations.

However, once Raye broke free from Polydor Records and took control of her career, she shattered stereotypes and redefined success on her own terms. In February 2023, she independently released her debut album, *My 21st Century Blues*, which peaked at number two on the UK Albums Chart. The lead single, "Escapism," became her first UK number one hit and marked her debut on the US Billboard Hot 100. Her success culminated in 2024 when she made history at the Brit Awards, winning six awards in a single night, including Artist of the Year and British Album of the Year, surpassing records previously held by Adele and Harry Styles.

Raye's story is a testament to what happens when women in music refuse to be boxed in by outdated industry norms. When they break free from the limitations imposed by predominantly male decision-makers in record labels, they don't just succeed—they redefine the industry itself, making history along the way.

This level of dominance is not accidental; it is embedded in the very structure of the industry, where a small number of powerful corporations decide whose voices are amplified and who remains on the fringes. The same industry that initially stifled her is the one that continues to determine which artists receive airplay, promotional backing, and financial investment.

Raye's journey is just one of many examples of artists who have had to fight against a system designed to keep creative control in the hands of a select few. Her ability to succeed outside the major label structure highlights a broader issue—one that extends beyond individual artists and exposes a deep-rooted power imbalance.

The labels can contest this, but the data speaks for itself. Hard numbers reinforce just how much control a handful of major labels exert over airplay, industry support, and commercial success. The *Why Not Her?* 2024 UK Top 100 Radio Airplay Report lays it bare—showing exactly who was signed and who was not in the year's most played songs. (I'll let you decide if it's blatantly obvious, eh?)

- **Sony Music Entertainment (SME):** 34.15%
- **Warner Music Group (WMG):** 31.71%
- **Universal Music Group (UMG):** 26.83%
- **Independent Labels:** 2.44%
- **Joint Ownership (UMG/WMG):** 2.44%

Despite industry claims of fairness, these figures expose a system where independent artists and labels are overwhelmingly sidelined. Together, SME, WMG, and UMG account for over **92%** of the top songs—an undeniable concentration of power. These corporations serve as gatekeepers, dictating not only which artists receive airplay but who gets the resources and opportunities to build sustainable careers. Their grip on radio playlists, streaming platforms, and festival line-ups ensures the same names dominate, while independent and diverse voices struggle to break through.

My good friend Vick Bain, a tireless advocate for gender equality in music, has extensively researched these disparities. Her Counting the Music Industry report, published in 2019, found that:

- Only 14% of songwriters signed to publishers and just under 20% of artists signed to record labels were female.
- This underrepresentation persists despite women comprising nearly half of all music performance graduates.
- Systemic barriers—including unconscious bias, lack of role models, and a historically male-dominated industry—prevent women from advancing at the same rate as their male counterparts.

This isn't just about artists—it's about the infrastructure that dictates what the world hears. Radio remains one of the most powerful gatekeepers in the industry, determining which voices are amplified and which are silenced. Labels shape culture by deciding who gets the most marketing, PR support, and industry investment—key factors that influence radio airplay, streaming visibility, and ultimately, festival bookings. While they don't control playlisting or radio airplay directly, their relationships with DSPs (Digital Service Providers like Spotify and Apple Music) and radio station programmers, along with their ability to fund large-scale campaigns, significantly impact which artists receive prime playlist placements and consistent airplay. This, in turn, affects streaming numbers, media exposure, and live performance opportunities, reinforcing a system where the same names continue to dominate while independent and diverse voices struggle to break through.

The Disappearance of Independence

It is worth me noting here that while artists like Raye have shown that success outside the major-label system is possible, the industry continues to shift in ways that make independence harder to sustain. Just recently, one striking example is the acquisition of Downtown Music's assets by major players, further limiting the landscape for independent artists and songwriters. Downtown was once a beacon for those seeking to retain creative control while accessing essential services like publishing and distribution. But as its catalogue and infrastructure were absorbed by the very corporations that dominate airplay, streaming, and live opportunities, another door to true independence quietly closed.

This isn't just a business transaction—it's another step toward the increasing monopolisation of the industry. When the same few corporations control what gets heard, what gets funded, and what gets played, the cycle of exclusion deepens. The illusion of choice remains, but in reality, artists navigating the system have fewer alternatives than ever.

And if you thought those figures were bleak, consider how the infrastructure continues to shrink around independent artists. It's not just about who dominates airplay today—it's about who is allowed to build a future. The acquisition of Downtown by the majors further consolidates control, leaving independent artists with even fewer opportunities to retain their creative freedom and visibility.

If major labels continue to absorb or control the spaces where artists could once retain independence, then the fight for representation isn't just about changing radio playlists—it's about reclaiming an entire ecosystem.

Advocacy in Action

Equipped with this data, I worked to challenge the status quo. I presented my findings to industry gatekeepers, sparking difficult but necessary conversations about equity, representation, and accountability. It wasn't easy—many resisted the change, offering every excuse in the book to justify the status quo.

The impact was immediate. The Gender Disparity Data Reports in the UK and Ireland made headlines across major platforms, including **The Guardian, The Independent, Clash Magazine, RTE, and BBC**. These reports dominated media coverage, putting gender disparity in Irish and UK radio under a glaring spotlight.

From Industry to Governance

The impact didn't stop with the music industry. The report opened doors to conversations at the highest levels of governance. Political party leaders and gender equality committees invited me to meet, eager to address the systemic issues the data exposed. These were spaces where decisions about national policies and cultural priorities were being shaped, and the evidence presented in the report became an unignorable catalyst for engagement.

What began as a focus on radio airplay inequality in Ireland had grown into a movement that resonated across sectors and countries. Political leaders acknowledged that addressing gender disparity in creative industries wasn't just a cultural issue but an economic and societal one. Excluding women and marginalised voices wasn't only stifling creativity but also holding back entire industries from reaching their full potential.

The Human Element

During this time, I discovered that data alone cannot change people's beliefs. Numbers only become meaningful when translated into a compelling story. Data storytelling taught me that data, when contextualised with lived experiences and human emotions, has the potential to persuade and inspire.

One of the most impactful questions I've posed to powerful men across broadcasting and significant labels, simple yet personal, is this: *What if this were your daughter?* This question shifts the abstract into the individual, forcing them to confront the implications of inequity on a level that cannot be dismissed. This question humanises the data, making it impossible to separate from their experiences and values. In these conversations, the most profound moments came when men began to see the data not as abstract numbers but as reflections of their own lives. I remember one broadcaster pausing after I asked about his daughter. His face softened, and I saw the shift in his perspective. It wasn't just about statistics anymore—it was about his family, his legacy, and the world he wanted to leave behind. This is the power of humanising data: it transforms resistance into reflection, and reflection into action.

A Blueprint for Change

Understanding the facts is the first step toward consciousness, which leads to change. Facts alone are insufficient; they need to be combined with compassion, tenacity, and a will to confront embedded inequalities. This art is not about pointing fingers; it is about constructing bridges. The reports were more than simply critiques; they were blueprints, outlining specific strategies, offering actionable steps even, to break down the walls that had held so many people back. From redesigning radio playlists to broadening festival lineups, the idea was not to demolish what existed, but to reconstruct it in a way that acknowledged the contributions of all voices. Change is not easy, but it is always worthwhile. Using statistics to open doors and start conversations made me realise that when we face the truth and commit to improving, progress is not just possible but inevitable.

With this important work, each step forward brings us closer to an industry that values talent and artistry over bias and tradition. The journey to equity is more than creating space; it's about reimagining and reconstructing the foundations of our systems to serve everyone equally. This transcends the music industry. It's a blueprint for collective liberation—a vision where the power of unity, diversity, and shared purpose propels us toward a more inclusive world. And at the heart of this transformation lies the undeniable strength and indeed vast potential of women, whose leadership will, one day, light the path forward.

This path has always been about more than just discovering the truth or inspiring action; it's about reimagining what is possible. The data may have opened the doors, but by Jesus the countless conversations kept them open, and it was during those chats that I realised something fundamental. The fight for equity is more than just a professional endeavour; it is a deeply emotional reckoning.

For me, growing up in poverty, abuse, and dysfunction meant clinging onto the smallest glimmers of hope, clutching towards the wants of a better life with hands that frequently felt too small and too feeble. That's why this work is so important to me. It is not abstract. It's about survival. It is healing. It's an opportunity to ensure that others do not have to experience the same quiet and invisibility.

True power does not come from slick boardroom presentations or polished speeches; it comes from embracing our stories, no matter how messy or raw, and amplifying them with unshakeable bravery. It lies in daring to imagine a society where every voice matters and every narrative has a chance to be heard and celebrated. I don't care how highfalutin that sounds; it's the truth.

As this book continues on, I'll go over the measures I took to make this idea a reality. It was a moment that transformed my life in ways I never ever imagined, and I hope it inspires and resonates with others.

Chapter 5

THE BOUNDLESS POTENTIAL OF WOMEN

"I demand the independence of woman, her right to support herself; to live for herself; to love whomever she pleases, or as many as she pleases."

— Emma Goldman

I believe that the potential of women is limitless. Throughout history, women have always shown an innate ability to connect intuitively. This shared connection transcends barriers and obstacles, forming a network of strength, support, and collective purpose. Whether consciously recognised, we are all interconnected, part of a vast intersectional feminist family that thrives on mutual understanding and solidarity.

Some thinkers and writers describe this phenomenon as the "feminine mystique"—an unspoken, almost ethereal bond that unites women across time and space. Others envision the Creatrix, the archetypal self-aware woman connected to other women and feminine creativity's source. This synergy, though sometimes intangible, is both a wellspring of personal power and a catalyst for broader societal change.

Shifting Systems of Power

Despite this immense potential, historical economic systems, which allow for collective advancement, have excluded women. Men have long benefitted from structures of brotherhood that not only foster solidarity but also amplify their financial and professional success. This network shares wealth, opportunities, and influence among them, thus perpetuating their dominance across industries. Women have yet to achieve the same economic vantage point, as centuries of systemic inequality have denied them access to resources, education, and decision-making roles.

The tides are shifting. Social media and the influencer economy have opened new doors for women to assert their economic power and create platforms that amplify their voices. In this digital age, women can bypass traditional gatekeepers, leveraging platforms like Instagram, TikTok, and YouTube to build personal brands, generate wealth, and foster communities of support. Influencers like Zoë Sugg, Chiara Ferragni, and Huda Kattan have created empires by fusing entrepreneurship and authenticity, showing how women can change the laws of financial power in a patriarchal society. Through the hefty democratisation of access brought about by such platforms, women from a variety of backgrounds are now finally able to establish avenues where they can express their voices, share their narratives, and make money from their artistic endeavours. How wonderful is that? I'll take all the hope we can get.

Social media has become the great equaliser, a space where voices once ignored can now demand attention. But it's not just about visibility—it's about rewriting the rules. Women are using these platforms to dismantle traditional power dynamics, creating global movements like #MeToo and #WhyNotHer? that expose systemic injustices. These digital campaigns aren't just hashtags—they're lifelines, amplifying stories that would otherwise remain unheard.

This dynamic age of digital empowerment is more than just a fad; it's a kind of revolution. In ways that were previously impossible, women are utilising their platforms to teach the next generation, raise money for charities, and promote equality. Social media has evolved into a vehicle for systemic change as well as self-promotion, giving women the chance to influence cultural narratives in ways that suit them. Accounts held by women such as Viola Davis, Ijeoma Oluo, Jameela Jamil, and others are excellent examples of this.

While these developments are great to witness, it is essential to acknowledge the persistent inequalities faced by women of colour and those in marginalised communities, who encounter even greater obstacles to accessing these platforms and opportunities. Not all of us are as fortunate. Amplifying these voices is as crucial as celebrating broader successes, ensuring no one is left behind in this movement toward liberation.

It might seem exhausting—having to fight against the barriers life throws at us, no matter where we are in the world. And look, I get it—many people are just trying to get through their own struggles, and that's real. But the truth is, most of us still carry some level of privilege, and recognising that is key. Patriarchal societies don't just harm women; they harm everyone, including men. Toxic masculinity enforces the false notion that vulnerability is weakness, limiting emotional expression and personal growth.

Feminist advocacy isn't just about fighting for ourselves; it's about making space to uplift others. That's the whole point—building a fairer world for all, where no one is left behind. It acknowledges the struggles men face without dismissing or diminishing them. It challenges us to rethink power structures, dismantle privilege, and create networks of solidarity that transcend gender, championing a shared humanity.

Ours is truly the age of liberation, and women will lead it—not just for themselves but for everyone.

In the previous chapter, we discussed data's revolutionary power—how it exposed systematic injustices and compelled institutions to confront their inadequacies. But data is only one part of the puzzle. Change is not driven only by numbers; it requires people who are ready to lead, confront, and inspire. Women have historically led such initiatives due to their combined power and perseverance. This chapter delves into our limitless potential as well as the changes that are already taking place on our path to liberty.

Recognising Global Struggles

Back in the West, capitalism presents us with a paradox. It convinces us we have enough while whispering that it's never enough. We watch from a distance as forces in other parts of the world rape, torture, mutilate, and murder women and girls fighting for liberation and fundamental freedoms. Meanwhile, we grapple with our own manufactured insecurities: are we too thin, too fat, too loud, too opinionated, or too much? Are we still single, too "unapproachable"? Unless we conform to the perfect mould—don't speak out of turn, look ladylike, smile, and remain polite—we risk being dismissed entirely. This script, designed by men and perpetuated by marketing machines, keeps us shackled to a system that sells us the illusion of worthwhile ensuring our compliance.

While we get caught up in our insecurities, devastating realities for women persist across the globe. Look at what's going on in Afghanistan and Iran; women's rights are not just ignored—they are being systematically dismantled by oppressive regimes.

Since the Taliban regained power in 2021, Afghan women have been subjected to relentless restrictions, stripping away their basic freedoms. Over 70 decrees have been issued, targeting every aspect of their autonomy, rights, and daily existence. These are not just rules—they are calculated efforts to erase women's presence and voices from society.

Girls have been stripped of their right to education, forbidden from attending secondary schools and universities. Women are barred from working in most sectors, excluded from public parks, and even denied the freedom to travel without a male chaperone. Hell, they cannot even speak or sing in public. Heart wrenching. They are being silenced and erased from every walk of public life, confined to their homes—sometimes even without windows. In a significant move, the International Criminal Court has issued arrest warrants for Taliban leaders, including supreme leader Haibatullah Akhundzada, accusing them of crimes against humanity for their systematic persecution of women and girls. This marks a historic step forward in the fight for global justice and accountability. But how it will pan out, nobody knows. Even writing this is outright depressing, but here we are.

Women's rights in Iran remain abysmal. It's impossible to separate the struggles of women in Afghanistan and Iran from the broader fight for global equality. These aren't isolated crises; they're part of a global pattern where women's autonomy is seen as a threat to patriarchal control. The bravery of women in these regions isn't just inspiring—it's a wake-up call. Their resistance reminds us that the fight for freedom is ongoing, and it's our responsibility to stand with them, amplifying their voices and challenging the systems that seek to silence them.

Mahsa Amini's death in 2022 caused nationwide demonstrations after she was arrested by the so-called "morality police" for allegedly not wearing her hijab appropriately. "Zan, Zindagi, Azadi!"—"Woman, Life, Freedom!"—became a catchphrase that spread globally via social media and the streets. These demonstrations, led by heroic Iranian women, have been met with violent crackdowns. There have been reports of imprisonment, abuse, and even death. Women continue to stand up in the face of severe repression, displaying amazing courage.

In all of the unrest, there has also been cultural defiance. Mohammad Rasoulof, the Iranian filmmaker who has publicly criticised the regime and was in prison during the Mahsa Amini protests, secretly directed his new film, The Seed of the Sacred Fig, while behind bars. Since its release, the film has premiered at Cannes to critical acclaim and was later nominated for the Best International Feature Oscar after Rasoulof escaped from Iran. This tale of resilience parallels the bravery of Iranian women defying the regime's suffocating hold.

It's extraordinary to witness this courage from our phone screens, isn't it? Weird, even, to feel so connected yet so helpless. These global struggles are poignant reminders of the inequities women experience worldwide. Meanwhile, within Western societies, we hash it out over made-up insecurities and social niceties while women in Afghanistan and Iran battle tirelessly for their most basic rights.

Acknowledging their bravery is a start, but it is not enough. Their battles demand global solidarity and action. The question remains: How do we turn observation into meaningful support for these extraordinary women fighting for freedom?

A Tangled Paradox

The difference between these struggles and the pressures facing women in the West could not be more precise, and yet the strands of oppression are eerily familiar. Not only do patriarchal systems strive to control, demean, and dehumanise women, but they do so using various mechanisms that yield the same results all over the world. Afghan and Iranian women are risking their lives to restore even basic fundamental rights stolen from them, but so many women in the West are still in a kind of cage. We form our bars from self-doubt, impossible beauty standards, and pressure to remain in moulds created to keep us small.

This paradox isn't accidental—it's by design. The same systems that oppress women globally also fuel the insecurities that keep women in the West distracted and complicit. By turning our attention inward, these structures ensure we remain isolated, unable to unite against the larger forces of inequality. Recognising this interconnectedness is the first step in dismantling it. The freedom we profess to hold seems empty—a false binary of compliance and rejection, invisibility and scrutiny.

The difference in opinion leaves us paralysed. We act as voyeurs to the suffering of others, consumed by our insecurities and distracted by systems designed to maintain our submission. The patriarchy ensures our focus remains inward, sapping the energy needed to dismantle these structures.

Yet, seeing these shared injustices is the first step toward solidarity. Though the struggles may look different on the surface, their roots intertwine in the same control systems. Now is the time to lift the veil, reject complicity, and find strength in one another. Our work as campaigners transcends personal freedom; we must amplify the cries of those suffering greater injustices.

How Do We Begin?

Adopting a new-age feminist movement requires a thorough awareness of the economical, historical, and political factors that shape our differences. Our experiences may differ, but what we share is the power to overcome, heal, and stand together. And when you look at the numbers, it's impossible to dispute.

According to the Central Statistics Office (CSO, Ireland, 2022), 28% of Irish women experienced some sort of sexual harassment in 2021, with younger women (18-24) suffering the highest rates. Keep in mind that this applies solely to those who report it. As if being young and navigating the world wasn't difficult enough, huh?

In England and Wales, the data inputs are even more concerning—the Office for National Statistics (ONS, UK) revealed that over 798,000 women were sexually assaulted in the fiscal year ending March 2022, accounting for around one in every thirty women

(ONS, 2022). Isn't this a terrible data input? Every time I read up on data, I have to literally check my fecking blood pressure.

And this isn't simply a historical lesson; things became worse throughout COVID. While the globe was closed down (and certain politicians were busy throwing office parties), abuse and harassment increased dramatically**.** In Ireland**,** 50% of young women (18-24) reported experiencing sexual harassment during the pandemic (CSO, 2022). (Jaw to the fucking floor).

Meanwhile, over the river in the United Kingdom, things were not looking good either. According to The Guardian, violence against women on public transportation surged by more than 50% between 2021 and 2023, with sexual offences rising 10% and harassment reports doubling. Because apparently, a pandemic wasn't enough—women had to endure additional harassment merely to go from A to B. (It is perfectly ok if you gather the urge to throw the book across the room at this point, it won't break, and you can pick it back up and resume as you were).

I want to emphasise again: these aren't just numbers—they're a damning indictment of the world we live in. But if stats alone could fix things, we wouldn't still be talking about this, would we?

Even in shared trauma, we find common ground. These figures aren't just statistics—they're a loud, undeniable reminder that solidarity isn't just possible, it's necessary. Because if we don't fight for change together, who will?

Change starts with awareness and vulnerability. We must dismantle the biases that hinder our progress and challenge the patriarchal narratives that bind us. And I'll say it again for good measure—as long as men claim leadership by dismissing women as 'too emotional,' 'too sensitive,' or 'too soft,' the rules of white male dominance will persist**.** As Emmeline Pankhurst stated, 'Men make the moral code and expect women to accept it.' It is time to **rewrite** that code.

The Power of Finding Your People

Together, we rise more potent and faster than ever. Find your people. Build your community. Embrace change; its value offsets its difficulty.

Understanding oppression, even in its intricacies, is not enough. Recognising the systems that perpetuate inequalities is only part of the equation. The true challenge lies in confronting those head-on. It demands action—a willingness to turn awareness into transformation.

For me, that click didn't come in a single, earth-shattering moment. It unfolded over time, as I began to question the industry I had spent years building my career in. The industry I loved was deeply complicit in perpetuating these inequalities. Slowly, but undeniably, I was forced to confront the truth: if I wanted change, I couldn't wait for it—I had to be the one to start it.

This was my light-switch moment.

You see, awareness alone isn't sufficient. When I saw the industry's role in maintaining these disparities, I knew I had a choice: continue benefitting from a dysfunctional system or confront it head on. That decision signalled the start of a new chapter in my life, one in which data, advocacy, and collective action were my tools and as I said earlier – my weapons – in the fight for change. In the following chapter, we'll look at how this light-switch moment became a movement, translating personal conviction into public accountability.

Chapter 6

THE LIGHT SWITCH MOMENT

"When a man gives his opinion, he's a man. When a woman gives her opinion, she's a bitch."
– Bette Davis.

In the previous chapter, we explored the boundless potential of women and how cultural shifts are beginning to create new opportunities. But potential and progress mean little without action. True change demands more than recognition; it requires a fire—a refusal to accept the status quo.

That fire was lit in me when I realised that the very industry I had worked so hard to thrive in wasn't just complicit in inequality—it was actively upholding it. This chapter delves into that awakening—the moment when everything I believed about my work and my purpose shifted.

Growing up in the 1980s with a single parent wasn't just a lesson in resilience—it was an education in systemic injustice. My mother struggled to raise her three daughters after her first son was taken from her when she was sent to a mother and baby home at just 18 years old. Our lives were shaped by the failures of a healthcare system and an unjust justice system, both deeply entangled with an antiquated Church and State that worked against women at every turn. Back then, I had no power to change anything. But those experiences planted the seeds of determination that would later grow into an unshakable drive to fight for equity and justice.

Fast forward to adulthood and my professional life; data didn't just give me clarity—it gave me power. In a world where opinions can be dismissed and lived experiences undermined, numbers are undeniable. They expose the truth, cutting through bias and complacency. I could finally demand accountability—not just for myself, but for every silenced voice in the industry.

But let's not romanticise it—this light-switch moment didn't strike like lightning. It started as a flicker, a gnawing unease about the walls I kept hitting and the ones I saw others smacking into, too. That flicker grew into a raging fire that burned through my fear and ignited a purpose that completely redefined my life. I am known for my bluntness by anyone who really knows me. Ask me a question and I will tell it as it is. So when I say activism isn't glamorous, I really mean that. It's messy, exhausting, and often thankless. But it's also necessary. Every time I was told to stay quiet, to fit in, or to accept things as they were, that fire burned brighter. Activism wasn't a role I chose—it was the only way I could live with myself. When you've seen injustice up close, staying silent feels like complicity. And for me, silence was never an option. Maybe I'm just that person who can never keep their mouth shut—if I see something wrong, I call it out.

The thing about activists is, most of us aren't born into the role. Activism isn't a calling—it's a necessity. It's what happens when life backs you into a corner one too many times, and instead of curling up, you come out swinging. That's how I see it, anyway. For me, it was enduring abuse on every level, nights of homelessness, wondering where I'd sleep, and surviving the volatile, violent chaos of my childhood. If I survived—and I did—it would either break me or make me.

Every part of my life led me here. Becoming an activist, a campaigner, was less of a choice and more of an inevitability. It was in my blood by the time I was 22, launching my own music PR and management company with little more than determination and a dream. The path ahead was a minefield. The industry wasn't welcoming—it was a gauntlet. Doubts and insults came thick and fast. One PR woman in Cork bluntly told me via email, "There is not a snowball's chance in hell you'll ever do anything in this business." A Dublin-based PR man decided to flex his metaphor skills, comparing me to a parked Lada while he cruised around in his shiny Formula 1 car.

Those words cut deep—but here's the thing: I'm a Taurus, and underestimating me is your first mistake. I printed out that Cork email and pinned it to my wall. It became fuel. I made a vision board filled with the artists and labels I dreamed of working with, and each rejection, each smug remark, only made me more determined to prove them wrong.

In those early years, I pushed myself to the brink. I am very competitive like that. I devoured every music industry book I could find—books mostly written by men who had no clue about perspectives like mine. My tiny bedroom became a cacophony of notes, research, and strategy. I was relentless. And then, as if the universe noticed, it threw me a lifeline.

One random day in the office, the phone rang. On the other end was a woman named Anette. She worked for Cooking Vinyl, one of Europe's leading independent labels, and after a few minutes, I realised this wasn't just a call—it was an impromptu interview for a role as their label and PR manager in Ireland. By the time we hung up, she'd offered me the job. And wow, did I hit the ground running working with that woman.

Anette wasn't what you'd call warm and fluffy—but she didn't need to be. Like me, she was a no-bullshit kind of woman, and unapologetically brilliant at her job. And I liked that about her. She cut through the noise of an industry dripping with pretence and proved that women could hold their ground, unflinching. What bonded us, though, was our shared love of cats—a fact that brought a softness to our conversations amid the flow of the non-stop.

Working with Anette helped to shape me professionally. It wasn't just that job; it was the people like her who taught me how to survive in an industry that felt designed to exclude people like me. The music industry wasn't always kind, but it taught me more resilience, and that became a lesson I carried into every campaign, every report, and every fight for change years later.

The pay for working in that label? Laughable. €375 a month, plus the odd expense for sending out physical stock. But the lessons? Priceless. Anette, for all her sharp edges, taught me the intricacies of global PR, marketing and collaboration. Over the few years that followed, I worked the PR for many label and management clients on campaigns for artists I'd grown up listening to as well as rising global acts—The Prodigy, Groove Armada, The Cult, Joss Stone, Lucy Spraggan, Ocean Colour Scene, Counting Crows, Taylor Momsen, and songwriters like Ron Sexsmith, Suzanne Vega, and Patty Griffin to name just a tiny fraction.

Eventually, though, in relation to Cooking Vinyl, the time came for me to move on. My request for a pay rise was turned down, and I knew I had outgrown the role. My client base had expanded, and it was clear that staying wouldn't align with my trajectory or my morals. The amount of time I was giving to a role that paid so badly was actually costing me money. They also had Marilyn Manson on their label and I didn't feel right continuing to work on his music releases. Still, the parting conversation with Anette was telling. Her words—"The industry is a small place Linda"—felt less like advice and more like a veiled reminder of the unspoken rules of the industry. Asking for what you were worth could see you edged out, yet there was an expectation to leave quietly, maintaining the facade. She then added, almost as an afterthought, "Well, we follow each other on Facebook, so I guess we'll still be connected somehow." I had given more than 5 years of my life to that client. I was utterly replaceable.

It was a bittersweet moment. Her comment spoke volumes about the transactional nature of the industry, where connections were more about maintaining appearances than genuine solidarity. Still, it served as a pivotal moment for me, sharpening my resolve to carve out my path and advocate for better conditions, not just for myself but for everyone working in this often ruthless field.

During that time, I put in many hours for various labels, management firms, booking agencies, and festivals. It wasn't just about establishing my worth to others; it was also about proving to myself that I belonged in those rooms—at those radio stations, record labels, album launches, gigs, and VIP areas—the spaces I once believed were reserved for others who, at first, may have been deemed 'better' than me. **Sidenote:** We are all the same. We live, and we die.

Working with Anette—and her tough, no-nonsense approach—helped me recognise that I didn't merely fit in. I was a power in my own right. And this was just the beginning.

By the time I was 32, I was at the top of my game, recognised as one of the leading music consultants and PR specialists in the UK and Ireland and my god, did I work hard to get to that place while working for pittance. But here's the head melt: the higher I climbed, the more I saw the industry's rot. Sexism, racism, and systemic inequality weren't just hanging by a thread—they were the damn solid foundation.

And I couldn't unsee it.

The light was on, and there was no turning it off.

That period in my life changed everything. It pushed me to ask myself hard questions and seek solutions that reached beyond my own career. In the next chapter, we'll explore how it grew into a movement, turning the fight for equity in the music industry into a model for change across sectors.

Chapter 7

DIVING INTO THE DATA

"Data is not just about numbers; it's about the lives and realities they represent. The real power lies in what we do with it."
– Dr. Catherine D'Ignazio, co-author of Data Feminism

Data is more than just numbers; it is a mirror that reflects the inequities ingrained in our systems. In this chapter, we'll explore how the revelations from the Gender Disparity Data Reports exposed systemic exclusion and catalysed conversations, from UK radio stations taking strides towards equity to the disheartening stagnation across the Irish Sea. The data tells a story of progress, resistance, and the urgent need for change.

It took four years after the initial series of radio reports to witness a significant shift in gender representation on UK and Irish radio playlists. In 2024, female artists achieved a historic milestone, comprising 41% of the Top 100 songs on UK radio—ahead of male artists at 39% and collaborations at 20%. This progress reflected a substantial cultural shift towards inclusivity and diversity in the UK music industry. I was delighted to be able to congratulate industry leaders like Jeff Smith of BBC Radio 2 and Samantha Moy of BBC Radio 6 Music, as well as the other networks across commercial radio, for their efforts. Being invited onto BBC Woman's Hour to discuss these findings as a guest alongside the legendary Chaka Khan was a surreal moment. It was a celebration of progress—a testament to what happens when the industry collectively decides to do better.

Unfortunately, that celebration did not extend across the Irish Sea. While the UK embraced these findings as an opportunity to innovate, Ireland seemed determined to stay in the past. The data exposed a massive divide: in 2024, Irish radio playlists remained nearly impenetrable for female artists. It was as though the industry had built walls too high for even the most talented women to scale, leaving their successes celebrated everywhere except at home. For reasons that continue to baffle both myself and my entire team, Irish radio remains stubbornly resistant to meaningful change. Year after year, we analyse the data, hoping for signs of progress, only to find the same grim reality staring back at us.

Our June 2024 report revealed a particularly sobering statistic: a mere 2% of the top songs that year on Irish radio were by Irish female artists. Jazzy leading that force—a lone beacon in an otherwise desolate landscape for women in Irish music.

Let's focus on Jazzy for a bit—because what she achieved was kind of historic. In May 2023, she dropped her debut solo single, 'Giving Me', released on March 10, 2023, under Polydor Records. The track, produced by Belters Only and Mark Ralph, soon became a hit.

The song went to number one on the Irish Singles Chart on May 19, 2023, making Jazzy the first Irish female artist to reach number one in over 14 years. That's not all; 'Giving Me' also topped the Spotify Ireland Top 50 Chart, marking the first time an Irish female artist had achieved this since the platform launched in 2012. Yeah, you heard that right—Spotify has been around for over a decade, and it took until 2023 for an Irish woman to get that top spot. Wild.

Jazzy's success wasn't just a personal win; it was a cultural moment. It showed, loud and clear, that when women are actually given airtime, their music resonates—big time. Her achievements shine a light on the talent that's been here all along but has been consistently sidelined. It's not about a lack of skill or creativity; it's about access and opportunity.

So, while the numbers in our report were bleak, Jazzy's success was a sign of hope—a reminder of what can happen when the door is even slightly cracked open. Now, imagine what the charts would look like if the playing field were actually level. The talent is here. The audience is ready. The only thing missing? Equal access to the airwaves.

What makes this even more disheartening is that 2024 was a year of extraordinary success for Irish female artists. Orla Gartland, CMAT, RuthAnne, Biig Piig, Muireann Bradley, Pastiche, Erica Cody, Soulé, Aby Coulibaly, and countless others were trailblazing across every other domain of the music industry. They were selling out arenas, dominating festival lineups, headlining tours, signed to major labels, and gracing international stages on prestigious TV shows such as Jools Holland, The Tonight Show, James Corden and Graham Norton. Yet despite their undeniable achievements, Irish radio stations still seemed to collectively shrug them off with rejections of consistent heavy rotation playlist inclusion. It appears that Irish women just aren't good enough to support. An outrageous sentiment that feels both archaic and deeply frustrating, but the data doesn't lie.

The broader findings further highlighted the systemic nature of the issue. Irish radio playlists remain overwhelmingly dominated by male artists, with many stations boasting playlists that featured not a single female artist. Some networks defended their choices, claiming audience preferences dictated the playlists. However, this reasoning falls apart under scrutiny; audience preferences are shaped by what they are exposed to, and Irish radio has consistently failed to create an equitable platform for female and marginalised voices to be heard.

When confronted about the lack of Irish female representation on radio playlists, the responses from heads of music at radio stations across Ireland were infuriating. These statements weren't just dismissive—they exposed an entrenched culture of complacency and bias. By deflecting responsibility, these music heads reinforced the barriers women face in an industry where gatekeeping is disguised as audience preference. Their excuses insulted not only the intelligence of female artists but also revealed the industry's reluctance to confront its role in perpetuating inequality. These weren't thoughtful reflections or genuine efforts to address the disparity; instead, they were a litany of excuses, dripping with sexism and deflection. The statements ranged from patronising to outright absurd:

- "Men make better music than women."
- "Why are you feeding us to the wolves?"
- "We don't have the budget to be diverse."
- "We don't make the rules."
- "Women just moan."
- "She's too old and long in the tooth to be making music."
- "We actually had some women on a special Friday night show back in February."
- "It's the label's fault, not ours."
- "It is whatever makes the charts."
- "People prefer to listen to male acts; they request them on air!"
- "You need to be careful and stop stepping on people's toes in radio."
- "You need to stop asking questions."

These comments didn't just reflect a lack of accountability—they laid bare the deep-seated biases that continue to exclude women from Irish radio playlists. They weren't merely passive aggressive; they were a brazen, real-time denial of the idea that women deserve equal airtime.

On many occasions, when speaking to Heads of Music—particularly in Irish radio—whenever I suggested they play more female and diverse artists, it was met with the kind of reluctance usually reserved for tax audits and cold sea swims. So, one day, just to gauge the level of their resistance, I threw out a half-joking suggestion: *Why not at least play them during the graveyard shift?* You know, the prestigious 12 midnight to 6am slot, when Ireland's most dedicated audience of night-shift workers, insomniacs, and the occasional fox rummaging through bins would be listening.

To absolutely *no* surprise, they *loved* this idea. They were practically beaming at their own progressiveness. A trial period was swiftly arranged—a groundbreaking initiative where women and Black artists could now grace the airwaves… while the rest of the country was unconscious. It was equality at its finest: *out of sight, out of mind… but hey, technically, we played them!*

I mean, who needs drive-time airplay when you can be the soothing background music for a petrol station attendant on the M50 motorway?

The patience it took to endure those conversations, engaging with music heads determined to deflect rather than listen, is something I still can't fully explain. This ingrained culture of excuses illustrates why progress has been so painfully slow and underscores the ongoing fight for gender parity in Irish radio.

These contrasting outcomes between the UK and Ireland reveal not just varying degrees of progress but fundamentally different attitudes towards accountability. In the UK, the data reports catalysed open conversations and tangible reforms. In Ireland, the same data seems to fall on deaf ears, perpetuating the exclusion of female artists from achieving the visibility and airplay they deserve.

The Irish Examiner aptly described the landscape as evidence of "systemic gender inequality" upheld by Irish cultural institutions. The article also noted that while progress had been made across other creative sectors, Irish radio remained stagnant—stuck in a time warp where women were "barely making music at all."

These outcomes highlight the urgent need for action, not just in Ireland but globally, to ensure that platforms like radio become spaces where talent, not gender, determines success. If the UK can make strides toward parity in four years, there's no reason Ireland can't follow suit—other than the reluctance of those in power to embrace change.

A Turning Point: Amplified Voices

The reaction to the reports was swift and far-reaching as we continued to release them over the last few years. Women's organisations, feminist collectives, and music groups rallied behind the findings, sharing them widely. The results weren't surprising for many women in music; they had long faced rejection, but the reports gave them a unified platform and renewed hope for change.

Male musicians and bands also came forward, offering solidarity and reflecting on their privileges. Conor O'Brien of Villagers admitted:

"I've had to dig deep in the last couple of years to truly comprehend the privilege I've taken for granted. I didn't see it in my 20s and early 30s because patriarchy and its psychological consequences are insidious and omnipresent... This report presents an opportunity for Irish radio stations to become a force for positive change, instead of perpetuating cycles of inequality."

Alfie, originally from the folk duo Hudson Taylor, expressed discomfort at noticing all-male lineups and playlists:

"I've tried to call it out, but it's not enough. The people in charge, and all the lads benefitting from this, need to talk about it and do more to change it, myself included."

Session musician and music director Sam Killeen commented:

"Misogyny strangles a woman's ability to make money and put food on the table. The radio stats prove that very little has changed. This needs to be addressed right now."

The courage of male artists to speak out against their own privilege is a crucial step in dismantling these barriers. Their willingness to reflect and act revealed an important truth: achieving equity isn't just a women's issue—it's a collective responsibility. When men in positions of power acknowledge their role in perpetuating inequality, they create space for meaningful change. I was deeply grateful for those who took that step, especially in contrast to the silence of the major male pop artists from Ireland who dominated the airwaves yet chose not to speak out.

Shocking Realities: Women's Voices

Female artists also spoke about their experiences. Imelda May articulated the struggles faced by women in music:

"How can a female artist have her music heard if she's not played? How can she reach success if people aren't even aware her music exists? My success shouldn't be proof that it can be done—it shouldn't be this difficult or biased."

RuthAnne, a Grammy-nominated singer-songwriter, echoed the frustration:

"The talent in this country is going to waste. This lack of representation doesn't just silence today's artists—it discourages the next generation of girls from even starting."

Eimear Noone, an award-winning composer and conductor, reflected on the systemic barriers:

"A creative professional cannot sustain a career without support. When opportunities are withheld, progress stalls. The impact is not just professional—it's personal. It stifles our creative hearts and minds."

Eimear was, of course, correct. It is disheartening, to say the least, when we are constantly met with closed doors. If we cannot see it, how can we become it? Young boys see their heroes everywhere in grown men who grew up knowing they could be whatever they wanted without the levels of criticism female artists endure throughout their careers. Women are judged endlessly on their looks, their relationships, their weight, and how they age. Did they age well? If so, it must be cosmetic surgery—and they're criticised for that, too. The man with a guitar will never get old; he becomes more refined, calmer, and wiser. Bob Dylan is a 'prime' example. On the other hand, women are told to give it a day, pack it in, that they've gone past their sell-by date. How glorious was it when Madonna proved all the ageist critics wrong?

On Saturday (May 4, 2024), in Brazil, Madonna broke records by performing for an audience of over 1.6 million fans, cementing her status as a performer who consistently breaks industry norms. The event, broadcast on the Brazilian network Globo TV, showcased her undeniable influence in Pop culture. What I loved about her performance was that it pushed back against the ageist and patriarchal standards that often set women aside as they grow older. Meanwhile, Mick Jagger is still celebrated for performing with the same swagger he had in his youth, a privilege rarely afforded to women in the industry.

While Madonna didn't comment specifically on her groundbreaking performance in Rio's Copacabana Beach, her stance on ageism and misogyny has been a consistent theme throughout her career. During her 2016 Billboard Woman of the Year acceptance speech, she stated:

"Thank you for acknowledging my ability to continue my career for 34 years in the face of blatant sexism and misogyny and constant bullying and relentless abuse."

In response to criticism about her appearance at the 2023 Grammy Awards, she added:

"Once again, I am caught in the glare of ageism and misogyny that permeates the world we live in."

Her comments perfectly capture her enduring resistance to the societal constraints placed on women, particularly as they age.

During the concert, Madonna invited Kylie Minogue to join her, delivering a performance that reflected their shared respect and support. This moment highlighted the ongoing struggle for older female artists, particularly regarding securing airplay. BBC Radio 1, for instance, has been criticised for sidelining female musicians over a certain age. Kylie has also faced similar treatment from stations like Capital FM, focusing on younger demographics.

Despite these obstacles, Kylie has remained committed to her music. Her single "Padam Padam," inspired by Édith Piaf's 1951 song of the same name, found success, reaching the top 20 in the US, number 23 in the UK, and topping the "UK Big Top 40," a chart that blends Apple Music streams and iTunes sales, back in 2023. I was delighted for her.

Madonna and Kylie show that persistence and creativity can break through biases, even in industries that have historically undervalued women as they age. Their achievements challenge outdated norms and pave the way for future generations, making it clear that women can and should take up space—at any age. Their achievements resoundingly rejected the stereotypes that persist in the industry and society at large.

These women are living proof that age and gender should never define an artist's worth or capabilities. Their resilience sends a powerful message: creativity transcends societal expectations. In their defiance, they don't just reclaim space for themselves—they extend it to every woman who has ever been told to sit down, to quieten her voice, or to fade into the background.

Just as Madonna and Kylie challenge societal norms on a global scale, there are women who have fought and continue to fight battles behind the scenes. Having unapologetic women around me with whom I could share my fears when they cropped up was invaluable. My good friend, author of *Anything For A Hit*, and a powerful advocate for women in music, Dorothy Carvello, once told me, "Part of being an activist or culture changer is being a disrupter." We cannot stop overthinking and worrying about how the truth will be perceived and received. That's what abusers want us to do—to stay quiet and afraid. Therefore, we must mute the background noise of concerns in our brains that stem from a cultural indoctrination that tells all women their voices don't matter. Change can only come from stepping outside of all that noise.

I had the privilege of interviewing Dorothy in 2021 on my podcast, *Why Not Her?*, and the journey spanning her career was almost unbelievable. The pages of her story are wrought with accounts of abuse and overbearing toxic masculinity in the workplace—and yet, it was all too familiar. During our interview, she told me she was proud to have been fired from every job she ever had in major labels and the music business because she always stood up for herself. When she was tired of putting up with the sexual harassment and mistreatment she alleges took place, and when she spoke up for herself, she said they would fire her.

All of these experiences she has written about in her book feature iconic male figures in the music business who controlled much of the industry as we know it. Men such as Doug Morris (an American record executive, former chairman, and CEO of Universal Music Group and Sony Music Entertainment) and Ahmet Ertegun (co-founder and president of Atlantic Records, who discovered and championed many leading rhythm and blues and rock musicians) appear in her book on numerous occasions. Dorothy said it was a culture she hated, one that rewarded criminality, sexual abuse and assault, rape, stealing, and everything connected to corruption of power. Her powerful ability to question why so many got away with mistreating women and perpetuating abusive environments was awe-inspiring.

Dorothy's story is a reminder that systemic change is never easy, but it is always worth the fight. Her bravery, alongside the defiance of artists like Madonna and Kylie, shows us what is possible when women refuse to accept the constraints placed upon them. As we continue to confront these barriers, we must also celebrate the progress we've made and the voices that have paved the way for others.

Meeting women like Dorothy and becoming friends with them along my journey as a campaigner has been instrumental in maintaining a positive mindset. I've also never met another human who used the word **'fuck'** in as many ways—or as often—as I do. We are kindred.

Never be afraid or too shy to reach out to fellow feminists and activists. It's a welcoming community. Faltering along the way is normal, but don't let it stunt your growth or your work. Take a break, reset, and come back to it when you're ready.

Madonna and Dorothy both exemplify that the fight for women's power—in music and beyond—requires resilience, disruption, and solidarity. Their stories remind us that when women take up space unapologetically, they pave the way for others to follow, ensuring that change ripples far beyond one individual's actions. Together, we can challenge systemic barriers and build a world where opportunity, equity, and respect are not privileges but rights.

The journey is a continuous one. Every report, conversation, and act of resistance adds to the momentum of the last.

Chapter 8

DRIVING CHANGE: THE PEOPLE AND THE PROOF

*"Never doubt that a small group of thoughtful,
committed citizens can change the world.
Indeed, it is the only thing that ever has."*

– Margaret Mead

This chapter brings together the people behind the movement. Over the last five years, volunteers and advocates from the fields of research and data science have poured their time and talent into this work without receiving a single cent.

Whenever you hear excuses like the ones I've heard—such as 'We don't have the budget' or 'Change takes time'—remember this: people-powered change is an unstoppable force. This movement has been shaped by remarkable individuals, each bringing their unique talents and ideas.

Here are some of the key experts and volunteers who worked with me:

Winnie Ama: Winnie, aka the true Lord Mayor of Belfast (in my opinion), is a powerhouse of talent, perseverance, and personality.

She's not just a star on stage; she's a diversity dynamo behind the scenes, constantly pushing for change in the music industry. Winnie's ability to juggle her music career with her advocacy work continues to leave me in awe—and a little suspicious that she might have discovered how to clone herself.

She's given countless press interviews on behalf of the campaign, often putting herself on the line to champion equality with a mix of grace, grit, and that signature Belfast wit. Behind the scenes, she's survived our Zoom marathons and WhatsApp brainstorms armed with caffeine, chaos, and a knack for one-liners that make data dives feel like stand-up comedy.

Winnie also mentors up-and-coming artists and hosts a weekly radio show on Colourful Radio, spotlighting fresh talent in the Future Soul and R&B scenes. We've spent more hours than I'd like to admit analysing data, crafting stories, and occasionally laughing at the absurdity of industry excuses.

Beyond music, Winnie is a data wizard and a Gender Pay Gap/HR specialist from Belfast. She's worked with hundreds of UK companies and helped develop an award-winning Gender Pay Gap product for Reed Business Information, empowering companies to identify, understand, and act on their gender pay gaps.

Winnie now works as a culture and technology consultant for a rapidly growing HR tech company in London. She's also one of the lead data analysts for Why Not Her?, playing a pivotal role in our groundbreaking reports and serving as a key speaker in our Diversity & Inclusion training sessions.

To sum it up: Winnie Ama is a one-of-a-kind creative force—a data-savvy, soulful singer, and diversity champion who somehow makes the impossible look easy. And if Belfast ever needs a badass mayor who can get things done? My vote's on her.

Other notable mentions go to our research team:

Gary Lynch: Head of Insights at Olytico with a background in social data analytics. We are lucky to have Gary as a seasonal volunteer with Why Not Her? as a data analyst and researcher.

Jennifer Williams: A data scientist passionate about using statistics to address societal issues. A recent graduate of UCD, Jennifer brings her analytical expertise to champion gender equity through data research on our reports.

Dr Michael Lydon: A Postdoctoral Researcher at UCC and a former lecturer in Popular Music Studies. Michael authored the influential *Uneven Score* report, supported by Sounding the Feminists, and is a volunteer researcher and data analyst with the above team members in Why Not Her?.

All in all, the work of driving meaningful change is never accomplished in isolation—it takes a community of courageous, compassionate, and committed individuals. Among these incredible allies over the years are people like Áine Tyrrell, RuthAnne, Aoife Scott, and indeed Winnie, who risked their careers to speak out in the press, on television, and across media platforms. Their bravery ensured that others—particularly those silenced or marginalised—might feel seen, heard, and validated. They lent their voices not just for themselves but for a collective betterment, sacrificing personal comfort to create a safer and more inclusive space for all. I am in awe of mná. Go raibh míle maith agaibh go léir!

Other remarkable individuals also deserve recognition for their time, expertise, and support. Dr Brenda Donohue, Bernadette Sexton, Pauline Scanlon & Karan Casey from the FairPlé Collective, Cian Sullivan, Vick Bain from The F-List, Eve Horne from We Are The Unheard, and Margaret E Ward each brought unique professional insights, volunteered hours of labour, and provided critical feedback. Many offered their "eagle eyes," ensuring accuracy and impact in every effort. Nadia Khan, a music consultant in the UK, also contributed to the first UK report I published—a one-off collaboration. She provided valuable insights and contributed statistics on Producer/Songwriter credits, enhancing the report's depth and reach. I only ever worked with her that one isolated occasion.

This group of people exemplifies the essence of community-driven change. Showing what can be accomplished when a group gets together motivated by a common goal and a refusal to accept the existing quo. Their contributions highlight the idea that advocacy is more than merely raising issues; it is about bringing together people who are prepared to take risks, share their skills, and stand in solidarity with one another. They demonstrated that dismantling old systems and building something better requires a collective effort. And I want to reiterate that they all gave their time, like I did, **for free.**

Now, let's take a look at some of the findings.

Findings On National Radio In Ireland from 2019- 2024

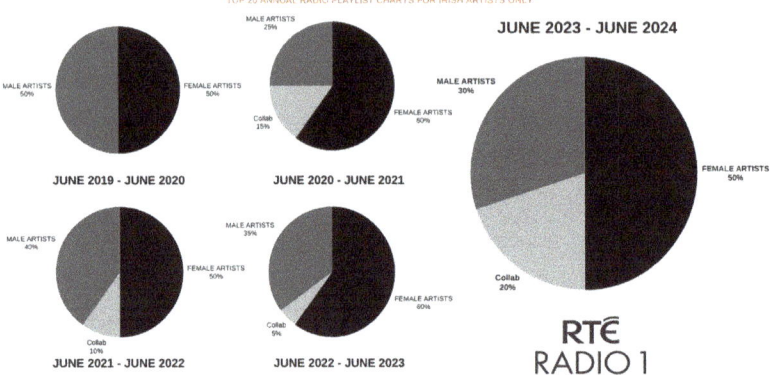

Graph 1. Shows National radio station, RTÉ Radio 1, in a five year period. They remain the most gender equal station in Ireland.

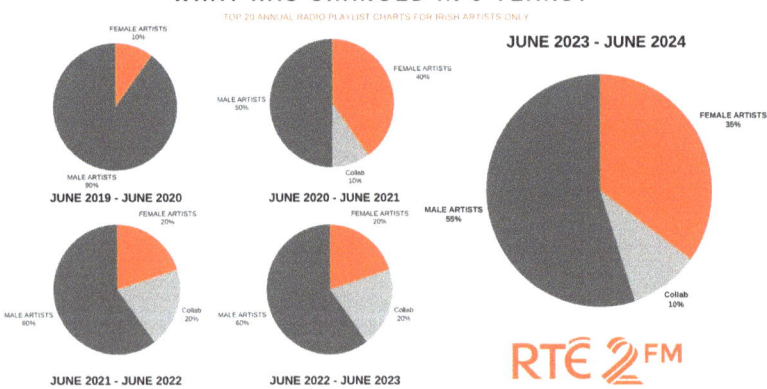

Graph 2. Shows National radio station, RTÉ 2FM, in a five year period. It should be easy for them to follow their sister station RTÉ Radio1 and reach gender parity. Tax Payers money contribute to this National Station. Women make up half the population. Why are they not including them fairly? We eagerly wait.

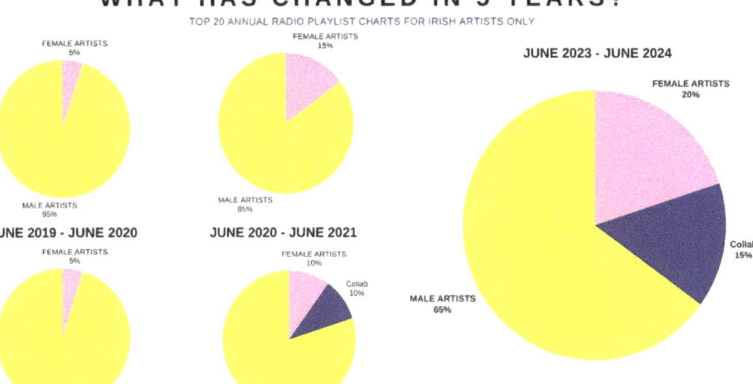

Graph 3. Shows National radio station, Today FM, in a five year period. I will just let the data speak for itself here.

National Radio Stations: RTÉ Radio 1, RTÉ 2FM, and Today FM

Among the national broadcasters, RTÉ Radio 1 has consistently maintained the highest percentage of Irish female artists, fluctuating between 50% and 60% over the five-year period. This demonstrates a relatively stable commitment to gender balance.

Martina McGlynn, Senior Producer at RTÉ Radio 1 and a member of the playlist committee, stated:

"We strive for quality throughout our music schedules on RTÉ Radio 1. We really are spoilt for choice as there is so much wonderful Irish music out there right now. Nevertheless, we are acutely aware of, and remain very mindful of gender-balance and diverse representation across the music that we schedule. Ultimately, all of our presenters play a pivotal role in bringing a wide range of music to our listeners chosen for its distinct quality, and I'm delighted to see that quality represented equally in both female and male artists. Going forward, we will continue to strive towards equal representation across our music schedules."

RTÉ 2FM, in contrast, has shown more volatility. The most significant improvement occurred between 2019-2020 (10%) and 2020-2021 (40%), marking a notable shift towards inclusivity. However, progress stalled in subsequent years, with a slight recovery to 35% in 2023-2024. Not good enough.

Today FM, is the least inclusive of Irish female artists, starting with an alarming 5% in 2019-2020 and saw only modest increases. Although it reached 20% in 2023-2024, it remains well behind other national stations.

These findings show the ongoing need for structural and policy-driven commitments to gender diversity in radio programming. While some national stations have made strides, others continue to lag, highlighting the necessity of sustained efforts to ensure female artists receive equitable airplay. Regional radio has been woeful, you can head over to https://whynother.eu/data-reports for a full list of all stations covered in the Irish radio reports to get the full evaluation and data available.

It is important to understand that these charts don't just represent numbers—they reveal the divide between stations committed to cultural change and those resistant to addressing the systemic exclusion of female Irish domestic artists. Behind these data points are countless women in Ireland's music scene who have been told, directly or indirectly, that they do not matter. For too long, they've been made to feel that their voices aren't as important as their male counterparts, that their work is somehow "not enough" to make playlists, and that the songs they write are overlooked simply because of who they are.

This is more than a struggle for airtime; it's a fight for recognition, respect, and equal opportunity. Every number on these charts represents years of rejection, resilience, and an unyielding determination to create in the face of systemic exclusion. These women are not just statistics—they are the soul of Ireland's music scene, fighting to be heard in an industry that too often silences them.

When I hear people saying, "Radio is dead," I can't help but scratch my head. Where are they getting these views and opinions from? The reality is the complete opposite, radio is alive and thriving, and the facts prove it. Every weekday, 3.36 million Irish adults (15+) tune into the airwaves, representing 80% of the population, with listening levels soaring to 90% some weeks. On average, audiences spend close to four hours (228 minutes) listening daily, particularly during peak times from 7 a.m. to 7 p.m. Local and regional stations capture a 52.5% share of this listening time, with national stations accounting for 47.5%. Even among younger listeners aged 15–34, 69.8% tune in daily, demonstrating that radio continues to resonate across all generations. Source: NLR/Ipsos MRBI Report (May 2024)

Radio isn't just alive—it's one of the most significant cultural and informational platforms in Ireland. The question isn't about its survival but about who gets to dominate its influence. The Irish radio industry, unlike its UK counterpart, has refused to evolve at the same pace. These charts serve as undeniable proof that structural discrimination in airplay is still very much alive—and that change will not happen without continued public and industry pressure.

But this isn't just an Irish issue. Now, let's take a closer look at the UK, where the data tells its own story of progress and resistance over the past five years.

Findings On National Radio In The UK from 2019- 2024

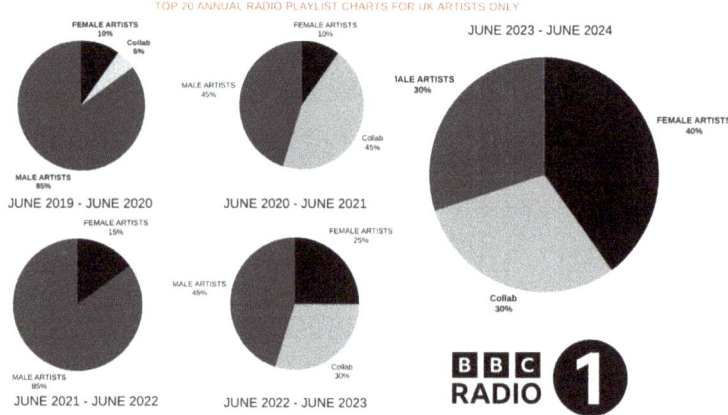

Graph 4. This chart showcases gender representation BBC Radio 1 over a five year period, revealing progress.

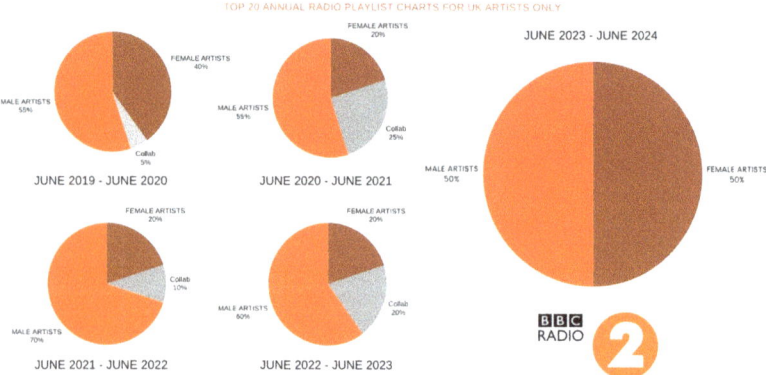

Graph 5. This chart showcases gender representation BBC Radio 2 over a five year period, revealing progress and their final reach towards total gender parity on their Top 20 rotation playlists. A huge milestone, setting the bar high across the entire network.

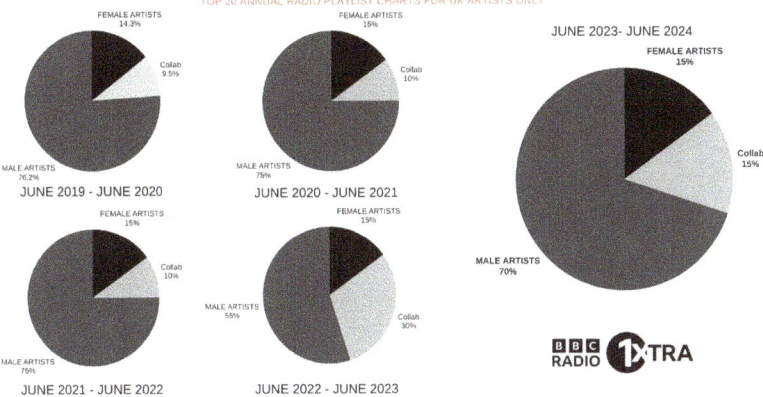

Graph 6. This chart showcases the lack of gender representation across the designated station designed to uplift marginalised voices within the black community of music creators on BBC Radio 1Xtra, over a five year period, revealing very little progress in gender parity towards black female artists and fronted bands.

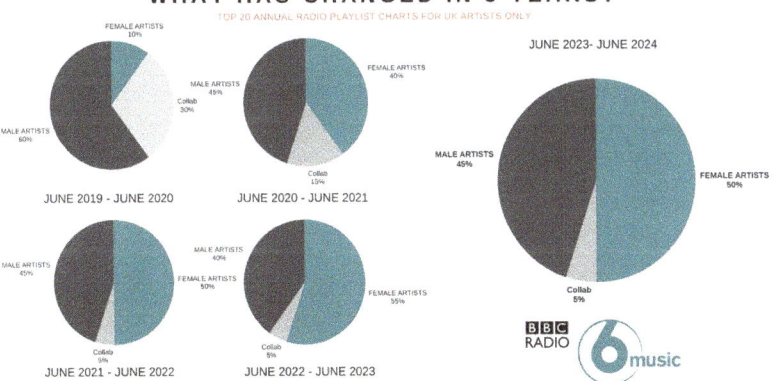

Graph 7. This chart showcases gender representation on BBC Radio 6 Music, over a five year period, revealing tremendous progress.

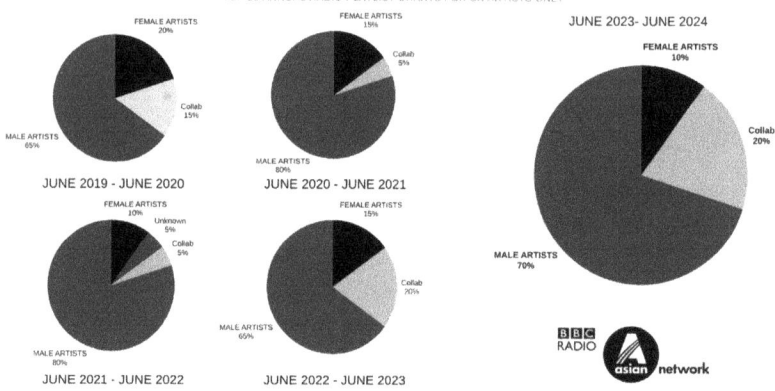

Graph 8. *This chart showcases gender representation BBC Radio Asian Network, over a five year period, revealing a significant lack progress towards female Asian artists and fronted bands.*

WHAT HAS CHANGED IN 5 YEARS?

Last year, we sent our congratulations to key stations within the BBC for embracing the ethos of their 50:50 Equality initiative (officially known as the BBC 50:50 The Equality Project). It is proof that when measures are made within an organisation to improve its DEI; it works! BBC Radio 6 Music, BBC Radio 2 and BBC Radio 1 lead with Gender Parity!

BBC Radio 6 has steadily increased the number of plays towards female acts on its heavy rotation playlists, achieving 50% gender parity in the most recent report for female artists. During this period, female artists/bands such as Wet Leg, Little Simz, Arlo Parks, and The Last Dinner Party have exploded onto the scene.

BBC Radio 1 has also increased support of female artists over the last four years, and last year, for the first time ever in our reporting period, BBC Radio 1 had more women in their annual Top 20 than men!

BBC Radio 2 finally reached total gender parity (50/50) on their playlist in 2024!

Again, as with the Irish reports, you can head over to https://whynother.eu/data-reports for a full list of all stations covered in the UK radio reports to get the full evaluation and data available. The stations mentioned here are just chosen to best illustrate the sways from progress to regression.

Rock and Roll... for Men Only?

It seems that three of the UK's most prominent rock, alternative, and indie radio stations—Planet Rock, Kerrang!, and Radio X—have collectively decided to act as if women-fronted bands are a mythical unicorn in the Rock and Alt/Indie world. You'd be forgiven for assuming that the idea of gender equality somehow missed their playlist meetings.

Radio X and Planet Rock, in particular, have been commendably quiet on the topic of gender diversity. You know, because silence is the most effective way to tackle inequality, right? Meanwhile, Kerrang! Radio made a *heroic effort* to acknowledge women in music—on the performative stage of International Women's Day, of course! Their Facebook post proudly declared:

> "On International Women's Day, we salute just some of the incredible female artists who inspire us daily. From legends to new voices breaking boundaries, their impact on the rock and alternative scene is undeniable."

Very touching, Kerrang! But here's the thing—if women are so inspiring "daily," perhaps consider celebrating them more than once a year? Radical idea: maybe even let them dominate your airwaves for a change. Rock radio stations love branding themselves as edgy, rebellious, and genre-defying. But their glaring failure to embrace gender diversity in their programming shows their true colours.

Let's take a closer look at the last 5 years of their Top 20 heavy rotation playlists from 2019-2024.

Planet Rock:

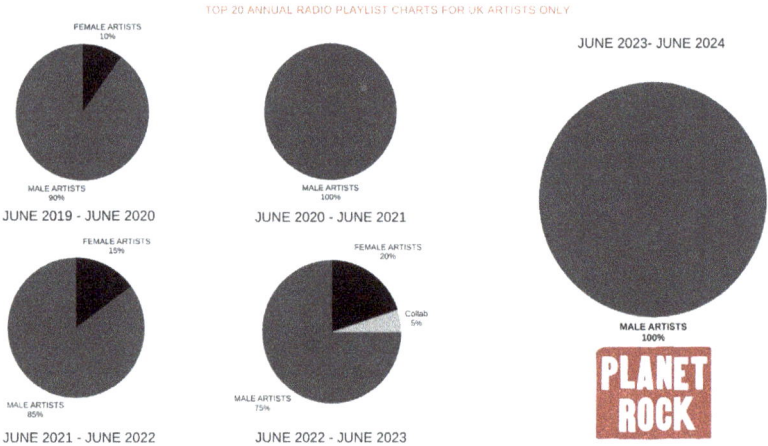

Graph 9. This chart showcases gender representation Planet Rock, over a five year period, revealing a significant lack progress towards female artists bands.

From 2019 to 2024, Planet Rock has shown a glaring lack of progress in gender representation, with white male artists continuing to dominate its playlists. This stagnation is particularly frustrating when the rock genre is thriving with an abundance of bold and innovative female-led talent. The Last Dinner Party, with their fresh and theatrical approach to rock, are making waves and captivating audiences with their unique sound. Black Honey's dark and cinematic approach to rock resonates strongly with modern audiences. Rising acts like Cassyette and YONAKA are proving that British female-fronted Rock/Alt bands are as fierce and innovative as ever.

Yet, Planet Rock seems determined to ignore these voices, opting to play it safe with the same male-dominated playlists. By doing so, they fail to represent the true diversity of modern rock and alienate a growing audience hungry for fresh perspectives. Representation is not just about fairness; it's about evolution. Rock as a genre thrives on rebellion and reinvention, and by excluding female talent, Planet Rock risks becoming stagnant and out of step with its listeners. The question is: when will they finally tune into the revolution happening right under their noses?

Kerrang! Radio:

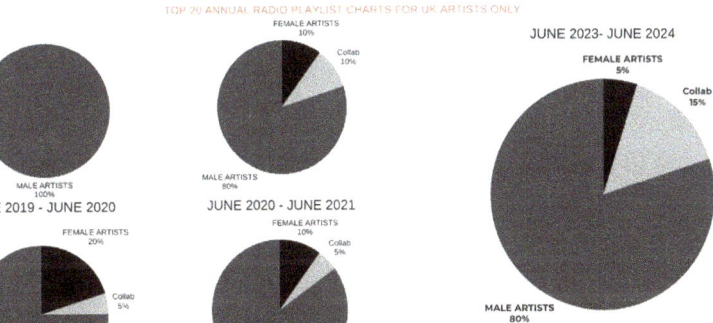

Graph 10. This chart showcases gender representation Kerrang! radio, over a five year period, revealing a significant lack progress towards female artists bands.

Kerrang! Radio has made some mild gestures toward inclusivity over the years. This lack of consistent progress feels particularly tone-deaf in a rock landscape where extraordinary female-fronted bands and artists are breaking new ground and amassing critical acclaim. Bands like Nova Twins**,** who seamlessly blend rock and punk, or Dream Wife**,** who challenge societal norms through their razor-sharp lyricism, are redefining what it means to be a modern rock act. Wolf Alice, winners of the 2022 BRIT Award for Best Group, have cemented their place as one of the UK's most successful contemporary rock bands. These acts represent a powerful evolution of rock music.

The question becomes unavoidable: how can a station that prides itself on amplifying alternative and countercultural voices remain so steadfastly rooted in the status quo? Representation isn't just a box to tick—it's essential for the genre's growth and relevance in a rapidly diversifying world. If this station truly wants to stay at the forefront of the rock scene, it needs to do more than pay lip service to inclusivity. It needs to start showcasing the incredible breadth of talent that already exists, including the fierce, innovative women leading rock into its next chapter.

Radio X:

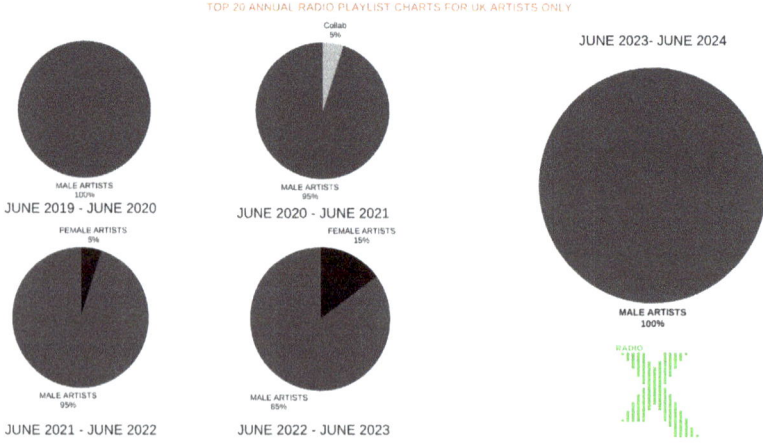

Graph 11. This chart showcases gender representation Radio X, over a five year period, revealing a significant lack progress towards female artists bands.

Radio X has fluctuated in gender representation, with male artists remaining dominant throughout the years. It is clear to see that one of the more prominent well-known and most listened to rock, alternative, and indie radio stations in the UK exhibit a disappointing lack of consistent progress towards gender diversity, with the predominance of white male artists overwhelmingly dominating playlists.

Efforts to integrate female voices and collaborations remain either temporary or absent. This shows that there is a vital need for a systemic overhaul in playlist curation to prioritise equity and inclusion.

Chapter 9

FOLLOW THE MONEY AND AMPLIFY YOUR INFLUENCE

"Whoever controls the media, the images, controls the culture."
— Allen Ginsberg

As Countess Markiewicz famously said, *"Dress suitably in short skirts and strong boots, leave your jewels and gold wands in the bank, and buy a revolver."* That fighting spirit embodies the work we undertook—not with weapons, but with data and determination. The momentum behind the reports was undeniable.

The reports ignited a fire that could not be ignored. What began as a grassroots campaign developed into a significant movement, drawing the attention of journalists, artists, producers, DJs, fans, and even politicians. When we shifted over to investigating the statistics behind political and news programming on Irish radio, we discovered that the discussions were no longer isolated to just the music business and the women in it; they were taking place all around. Women in politics were also being silenced off the airwaves.

Throughout this manifesto, one truth stands out: data storytelling has the power to ignite change. Numbers may reveal the truth, but when paired with human experiences, they demand action. That's exactly what I aimed to do—turn cold data into a human narrative that demanded accountability.

Building Bridges with Policymakers

As the voices grew louder, the next step became apparent: bridging the gaps. The reports had already captured media attention, but lasting change required structural action. I shifted my focus toward political leaders, TDs, and ministers.

I issued a press release urging the Irish government to address the gender imbalance in radio, capitalising on the momentum we gained after our campaign was featured in a 15-minute special on national television's RTÉ evening news. The coverage was robust, with interviews from incredible female artists and musicians adding more impact. The response was immediate, with prominent outlets like the *Irish Examiner* picking up the story and amplifying our call for change.

Over the course of the last five years of campaigning, I wanted to further understand who was shaping the music we heard as well as the entire cultural and political discourse filling Irish airwaves. The industry had long been skewed towards a dominant perspective, but how bad was it outside of music playlists? Joyce Fegan, a sharp and insightful journalist, revealed that 89% of morning radio hosts on regional stations were white men, dominating discussions on politics, current affairs, and social issues. These shows didn't just fill airtime—they shaped daily narratives, reinforcing a narrow perspective that excluded women, people of colour, and marginalised communities.

By leveraging the momentum from the media, we secured meetings with decision-makers, presenting the reports as tools to create healthier, more inclusive societies. For the hesitant, the media amplified the message, ensuring the issue couldn't be ignored.

The solidarity within the music community—artists, organisations, and now politicians—created an unprecedented sense of possibility. Together, we envisioned a future where women in music, whether in Ireland or elsewhere, were no longer silenced but celebrated.

The Pushback

When Joyce Fegan agreed to allow us to put her findings in a report through our collective, we knew the reaction would be intense—but nothing could have prepared us for the wave of backlash that followed the *Behind the Mic* report. The response from radio executives ranged from defensive denial to outright hostility. Some brushed off the findings, dismissing them as "incomplete" or "misrepresentative." Others took a more aggressive stance, calling the report "an attack on hard-working broadcasters" and accusing us of undermining the integrity of Irish radio. The more extreme reactions made it clear—we had touched a nerve.

But the most insidious pushback came disguised as concern—the meritocracy myth. One executive argued, *"We support equality, but we don't believe in tokenism. What happens when an underqualified Black woman takes a job from a more qualified white man? How is that fair?"* The privilege embedded in such statements was glaring, exposing an industry so deep in its own varying degrees of bias that it saw equity as a threat rather than an opportunity. It wasn't just reluctance—it was active resistance to change.

Who decided who was "qualified"? In a system that had spent decades excluding women and marginalised voices, the idea that "fairness" ever existed in the first place was laughable. The outright resistance—essentially a collective "What the actual fuck are you doing to us?!"—was proof of the problem itself. Gatekeepers weren't just reluctant to change; they were actively working to preserve the status quo.

"Meritocracy" became the excuse of the day, used to justify systems that had never been fair. It was exhausting to hear these tired defences when the evidence of inequality was right before them.

Opinions like these don't just dismiss progress—they obstruct it. Using Joyce's findings, we intensified our campaign by contacting advocates, pressuring decision-makers, and refusing to let the narrative be ignored.

Turning Point in Politics

The reports found their way into the Irish Parliament, The Dáil, thanks to allies like Holly Cairns from the Social Democrats, who presented the findings and demanded accountability. Other politicians followed, including Senator Marie Sherlock, Labour Party leader Ivana Bacik, and Sinn Féin Senator Fintan Warfield.

One of our most significant connections was with Minister Catherine Martin, an advocate for gender equality and intersectional policymaking. During her tenure as Minister for Tourism, Culture, Arts, Gaeltacht, Sport, and Media, Catherine was allowed to push for genuine change. In our meetings, she promised to prioritise diversity and representation, and her ongoing engagement with the reports brought hope that systemic reform was possible. Her leadership proved that progress is possible when policymakers take responsibility for dismantling the barriers women and minority voices face daily.

These moments showed that change is not just necessary—it's achievable. We were incredibly fortunate to have such a brilliant woman working with us and for us, rather than against us. This stood in sharp contrast to many other organisations, which, instead of fulfilling their responsibilities, actively worked against progress.

These moments were more significant than policies. They were about recognising the responsibility of those in power to dismantle systems that excluded women and minority voices for decades.

Following the Money

As I dug deeper into the data collected over years of reports in the UK and Ireland, I saw that the lack of diversity wasn't just cultural but structural. A handful of corporations control most radio stations, magazines, and advertising platforms.

- **Bauer Media**: Operating in multiple countries, Bauer owns KISS, Absolute Radio, and Magic Radio, as well as print publications like Heat and Grazia.
- **Global**: Europe's largest commercial radio company reaches 26.3 million listeners weekly in the UK alone through stations like Heart, Capital, and LBC.

This level of consolidation means that decisions made by a few executives have an outsized impact on the industry. While this centralisation often reinforces inequality, it also presents an opportunity. If these decision-makers commit to diversity, the effects could ripple across entire networks, transforming the cultural landscape at a much faster pace.

Building a Better Future

A single individual or group does not shape culture; everyone shapes it. But let us not pretend the playing field is level. A tiny group of media moguls, tech titans, and billionaires exerts power, controlling much of what we see, hear, and believe. It's the type of authority that feels dystopian rather than democratic. The notion that a single tweet from Elon Musk or a soundbite from Donald

Trump may cause tremors across economies and ideologies is remarkable and alarming.

Cancel culture may be as oppressive as unchecked authority from media moguls and internet titans. It discourages people from challenging the existing paradigm for fear of falling out of line. A society where everyone parrots the party line, regardless of ideology, is unsustainable. We progress in the grey zones through awkward and tough conversations.

We can create a space where diverse voices thrive by demanding transparency and accountability—not just from the powerful but from ourselves. Culture should celebrate talent, creativity, and authenticity—not confine them to an ideological box. The future we're building demands bravery, fairness, and a willingness to embrace diverse voices.

The reports, the data, and the voices of advocates have laid the groundwork. But the real question remains: how do we turn this momentum into lasting change? The answer lies in action—and that's where we're headed next.

Chapter 10

WHY NOT HER? TURNING VISIBILITY INTO VICTORY.

'The Master's Tools Will Never Dismantle the Master's House,'
– Audre Lorde

I am a storyteller armed with data and facts, using them to carve out spaces in an industry resistant to change. This isn't about algorithms or tools—it's about persistence: asking the right questions, demanding answers, and refusing to give up.

By this point, women and people of colour in the music industry may find the headlines and statistics familiar throughout this little book. The hard facts shocked audiences in Ireland and the UK, exposing the structural biases embedded in radio playlists, programming, and decision-making processes. The data omits the quiet conversations, unspoken doubts, and subtle victories. So I hope I have managed to shine a light on that.

One of the most important lessons I learned was that data alone cannot create change—it needs a human element. It's not enough to present statistics and expect transformation. Change happens when numbers meet lived experiences when outrage turns into action, and when those in power can no longer ignore the stories behind the spreadsheets.

Every time a radio station excludes a song by a female artist or an artist of colour, it's not just a missed opportunity for that individual—it's a loss for all of us. These are stories, perspectives, and ideas that leave a void in our culture, a silence where voices should be heard.

For aspiring female artists in Ireland and the UK, the lack of representation wasn't just disheartening but career-defining. Building momentum, securing gigs, or breaking into the international market without radio airplay became nearly impossible. The message was unmistakable: your voice matters less if you're a woman.

Beyond the Hashtag

Visibility was just the beginning. Viral campaigns and hashtags opened the door, but real change required stepping through it. Structural accountability was the only way to dismantle decades of inequality. The #WhyNotHer? movement ignited conversations, but conversations alone weren't enough to dismantle decades of ingrained inequality. The next step was clear: we needed to target policymakers, licensing bodies, and corporate decision-makers—the gatekeepers with the power to enforce change. Although, the data revealed what many women and people of colour already knew; it's true power came when it transformed from numbers on a page into stories that exposed systemic bias and demanded action.

We didn't just ask for promises; we demanded measurable action. Our relentless efforts bore fruit two years after the first report went viral. In October 2022, Minister Catherine Martin of the Green Party introduced legislative changes. These Online Safety and Media Regulations Bill amendments marked a turning point.

For the first time, the amendments promoted gender balance in broadcasting.

Minister Martin explained the significance of this move:

> *"Young girls cannot aim to be what they cannot see or hear. There needs to be a significant improvement in the ratio of women to men on radio and TV so that both genders feel represented in public discourse, and better representation of women in music on our airwaves."*

The bill empowered the newly established Coimisiún na Meán to introduce media service codes that prioritise gender balance—not just in news and current affairs programmes but also in music programming, ensuring that works composed or performed by women receive fair representation. The commission used to be the former Broadcasting Authority of Ireland, with whom I met regularly throughout the last few years until it was dissolved. Then, it was renamed the Coimisiún na Meán. They still give us the same empty promises, and they never once gave a public statement on why they failed to lead Ireland's broadcasting sector to plurality, equality, and diversity, despite spending a lot of money hiring some of the same people from the old BAI (Broadcasting Authority of Ireland). All that aside, on paper, it was an unprecedented step forward for Irish broadcasting, and the Green Party acknowledged the contributions of organisations like Why Not Her?, an unfunded volunteer collective, and the National Women's Council in shaping this legislation.

This legislative victory wasn't handed to us; it was earned through years of relentless campaigning, data-driven Advocacy, and an unwavering commitment to change. But we knew this was only the beginning. Legislation alone cannot transform deeply embedded systems—it requires vigilance, accountability, and continued pressure to ensure its implementation.

The journey from a viral hashtag to legislative action showed that real change isn't a moment; it's a movement. One report, conversation, and hashtag started the process, but the follow-through turns visibility into victory. For us, five years on, the work is still far from over. It is about ensuring that these policies are not just words on paper but transformative actions felt across every airwave and playlist.

New Frontiers

As the campaign grew, so did its scope. What started as a campaign for gender equity in Irish and UK radio quickly became part of a globalised movement. The data and advocacy sparked conversations far beyond the originally intended territories, resonating in countries like the Canada, France, Sweden, United Kingdom, Australia, the USA and Turkey, inspiring organisations in other countries to take action and join the conversation.

The Bigger Picture

This journey taught me that no system operates in isolation. Music, media, and politics are deeply intertwined, shaped by the same biases and power structures. To challenge one is to challenge them all.

For example, while some stations improved gender representation in their playlists, they failed to address racial diversity. The work isn't done until everyone has the space to be heard.

What comes next? The answer isn't simple, but is clear:

Accountability: Those in power must be held accountable, not just for their words, but for their actions.

Intersectionality: Change must be inclusive, addressing gender, race, sexuality, and all the intersections of identity.

Sustainability: Progress isn't about quick fixes; it's about building systems that prioritise equity for the long term.

The path forward demands persistence, accountability, and inclusion. It's not just about asking 'Why not her?'—it's about creating a world where the question doesn't need to be asked at all. Wouldn't that be grand?

Chapter 11

RESILIENCE AND RENEWAL IN A POST-COVID WORLD

> *Resilience: "The inherent ability of a system to modify its functioning before, during, and following a change or disruption so that it can continue necessary operations in both expected and unexpected situations."*
> *– From the Latin: resili(ēns), prp. of resilīre, meaning "to spring back, rebound."*

When my girlfriend asked me, 'If you could, would you take it all back?' my answer was immediate and unequivocal: 'No.' This work has changed me in ways I never could have predicted—teaching me more about empathy, sharpening my determination, and opening my eyes to the resilience required to fight for justice in an often resistant world. In doing so, I found a deeper understanding of the world and how people, particularly those marginalised—non-white, non-male, and often ignored—are treated. Our society segregates, alienates, and pushes these voices to the margins, leaving them silenced in industries that should celebrate their creativity and contributions.

Looking back, this journey feels like navigating a storm in the dark—trusting an uncertain path, even when every step felt like it could lead to disaster. It was perseverance, not clarity, that kept me moving forward. Maybe it was naivety, but I believed people would change because the truth was clear. Spoiler: They didn't. And perhaps that's the harshest lesson of all: change doesn't come from truth alone—it takes resilience, persistence, and an unwavering belief that the work is worth the fight. That's the essence of this movement—finding strength in the face of adversity, even when the obstacles seem insurmountable.

I've faced it all—trolling, silencing, and professional isolation. I've been called "filthy lesbian dyke," "man-hating bitch," and "fucking clueless." Some insults were thrown by industry professionals I had once respected. Even some women—conditioned by fear or driven by self-preservation—joined in. They later deleted their posts and tweets. It wasn't just words; it was a mirror of how deeply ingrained these biases are. This kind of trolling became like water off a duck's back for me. If I let it get to me, I would have stopped a long time ago.

I've learned that no matter how seriously or thoroughly you approach your job, you can never please everyone. And you know what? That is not your mission in life.

We aren't here to conform to someone else's idea of what is acceptable. Change doesn't happen by staying silent or keeping everyone comfortable. It comes from standing firm in your values, even when resistance feels overwhelming. Progress demands courage, and that courage often comes at a cost.

I kept the course not for recognition or affirmation but because I genuinely care about others. I trust humanity's potential to adapt, unlearn destructive behaviours, and recognise the incredible power of variety and inclusiveness. By listening, questioning, and learning, we can build a society that leaves no one behind—a world where justice is a lived reality, not just a goal.

The groundwork we had laid through reports, campaigns, and relentless advocacy bore fruit. The legislative changes introduced in Ireland, particularly the Online Safety and Media Regulation Bill, were a significant victory—but they were also just the beginning.

In the wake of those changes, the question shifted from "How do we achieve structural accountability?" to "How do we sustain it?"

Beyond Legislation

The legislative victories in Ireland were monumental. They created accountability frameworks for the media that had long been absent. But laws don't change cultures overnight. While stations like RTÉ 2FM and Spin 103.8 began to step up, others lagged behind, clinging to outdated practices and resisting real change.

This highlighted something critical: systemic change requires more than policies—it demands a shift in mindset. It's about accountability, monitoring progress, and amplifying those who lead by example.

Stations that embraced inclusivity saw immediate benefits. Audiences responded to the richer, more diverse soundscapes with enthusiasm, proving that variety doesn't just enrich the industry—it strengthens it. On a national level, RTÉ 2FM's switch to more diverse playlists wasn't just a box-ticking exercise; it was transformative. The same was true for the UK, where the BBC stations began to diversify their playlists, finally amplifying voices long silenced.

The Cost of Advocacy

Advocacy isn't just about perseverance; it's about accepting the personal and professional costs of speaking truth to power. Those costs can be heavy, and for me, they often were.

Take, for example, this lovely email I received from an anonymous account, 'headsuplinda@gmail.com.' It read:

Hi Linda

Just giving you an anonymous heads up and advice as a friend. Everyone in the industry has been talking about you and the activity around increased airplay for female Artists. Yes your views and opinions on this matter are correct and it is great to see and I admire you for it, however having said that you are stepping on people's toes and it has gotten to the stage where enough is enough.

The word is that if you keep stepping on people's toes and it is pushing into the stages where music directors, stations, and other outlets are going to blacklist/ignore you and this will result in your clients receiving no airplay or coverage. Speaking to a lot of the DJs and jocks they have heard enough about all this.

This is a friendly heads up as I admire you for it, but I also do not want to be involved either. Take what you like from this but as I said above it's just a heads up.

This wasn't just a warning—it was a calculated attempt to silence me. The message was clear: challenge us, and there will be consequences. And there were. But I refused to back down, knowing that this was bigger than me—it was for every voice that had been silenced.

What followed was professional isolation. Trolling and threats—both online and offline—became routine. People I once considered allies disappeared. And ironically, it wasn't even just the men who came for me the hardest—it was the women too. Women who built their careers on empowerment slogans, who could recite *Sisterhood is Powerful* in their sleep, yet the moment the fire got too close, they vanished like a bad date who suddenly "forgot their wallet." Turns out, *solidarity* had a small print: *only when it's convenient.*

But here's the thing: Advocacy isn't comfortable. It demands risk, confrontation, and sacrifice. I expected this, remaining resolute even when discouraged. This work was never just about me—it was for the countless women, artists of colour, and underrepresented voices who have been excluded for far too long.

Change requires discomfort for those demanding it and those who must face it. The backlash I endured wasn't evidence of failure but proof that the fight was necessary.

A Shifting Landscape

The legislative reforms of 2022 in Ireland, as well as the crucial work of many UK organisations right up to 2024, described in the Misogyny in Music study, were key milestones. The report of the UK Parliament's Women and Equalities Committee revealed the widespread obstacles that women experience in the music industry, such as gender discrimination, sexual harassment, and a persistent lack of assistance. The research emphasised that, despite significant improvements, the business remains a "boys' club," with women facing unreasonable barriers to opportunity and experiencing structural disparities.

Meaningful change required more than words—it demanded action. The focus needed to shift from promises to tangible outcomes, ensuring that industry practices aligned with the newly introduced measures.

The reaction was more than just resistance; it was terror. The gatekeepers were terrified as they saw their power and influence were slipping away. I'll say it again—progress is not about pleasing everyone; it's about dismantling systems that have historically silenced diverse voices and excluded fresh perspectives. Real progress creates opportunities for those who work hard, regardless of their gender, ethnicity, or background. And to those who roll their eyes at DEI (Diversity, Equity, and Inclusion) initiatives, labelling them as "woke," it's time to take a hard look at the privilege you're standing on.

The reality is that DEI is not about lowering standards or handing out giveaways; rather, it is about levelling the playing field, which was purposely constructed to favour a select few (white men). If you're screaming against these systems, you're really defending your comfort in a space that has historically excluded others. That comfort comes at the expense of skill, creativity, and innovation, which have the potential to enhance the sector. Diversity does not simply "accommodate" progress; it is essential to it. Without different views, the industry stagnates, resulting in an echo chamber that serves no one really, as everyone suffers in some way or another.

This is more than just doing the right thing; it is about survival. A creative sector that does not reflect the diverse backgrounds of its consumers will eventually lose relevance and legitimacy. The era of gatekeeping is ending, and what lies ahead requires perseverance, fortitude, and a firm commitment to a more equal and inclusive future. There is no turning back now—the path ahead is plain, and we are all responsible for walking it.

Audiences desire music that is reflective of the world they live in. Artists deserve equal opportunity to be heard. And we all deserve a cultural landscape that sees diversity as a strength, not a threat.

We have gone a long way, but the journey is far from over. These changes are only now having an impact on the cultural environment. The question now isn't whether change is possible, but how we sustain it for generations to come.

Chapter 12

WE DON'T HAVE THE BUDGET...

There's a saying: 'Excuses are the tools of the weak and incompetent.' Nowhere is this more evident than in the refrain, 'We don't have the budget'—an excuse I've encountered countless times in my advocacy journey. But excuses build nothing, and progress demands action, not avoidance.

This is a brief chapter, as it's also a short excuse. Advocacy work teaches you early on that change frequently faces a barrage of excuses. The reason I've encountered most frequently is this: *"We don't have the budget."*

This phrase became a constant refrain during countless interviews, meetings, and panels across Ireland, the UK, and beyond. To shield the status quo, radio stations and media executives used 'budget constraints' to explain their lack of diversity and gender disparities, respectively.

I've sat through Zoom calls with some of the most influential figures in the music industry, organisational, and political leaders—people with immense resources at their disposal—only to hear them insist that enacting change was too costly. Yet, I always wondered: costly for whom? When a marginalised artist can't gain airplay, can't book a festival slot, or can't advance their career, the executives don't bear the actual cost—the artists bear it.

To dismantle the myth of budget constraints, we developed the Gender Action Plan—designed to empower media organisations to implement meaningful change. The plan shattered every excuse for inaction, such as the persistent claim that budget constraints were a barrier to progress. With the exceptional Dr. Brenda Donohue and Bernadette Sexton, we developed an accessible, zero-cost framework that empowered radio stations and media organisations to implement gender balance and diversity measures. We presented this plan freely to radio stations and organisations nationwide, including the Coimisiún na Meán—Ireland's media regulatory body, 'which fosters a diverse, safe, and thriving media landscape'. (I don't think they got that memo). In doing so, we removed the financial barriers often cited as justification for a lack of progress.

This wasn't just a random trio of women cobbling something together. Let me take a moment to spotlight the incredible women who worked alongside me and made this possible.

Dr. Brenda Donohue: A Catalyst for Change

Dr. Brenda Donohue is a distinguished academic and researcher specialising in gender equality and cultural representation. Her groundbreaking work on Waking the Feminists and Gender Counts: An Analysis of Gender in Irish Theatre (2006–2015) uncovered systemic inequities and provided actionable roadmaps for change. With a career rooted in theatre and the arts, Brenda has long championed gender equity in industries plagued by imbalances.

Fun fact: Brenda and I first met in the car park of a SuperValu shop just after the COVID restrictions lifted. A brief chat evolved into a lengthy walk and a candid conversation concerning campaigning, mutual challenges, and female solidarity amidst hardship.

Brenda's exceptional skills in media and cultural studies played a crucial role in developing the Gender Action Plan. Her meticulous approach to data-driven solutions ensured the framework was robust, accessible, and designed to dismantle systemic barriers to diversity. Brenda's unwavering commitment to justice turned our vision into actionable solutions that inspired trust and confidence in the media sector.

Bernadette Sexton: A Global Advocate for Equity

Bernadette Sexton's extraordinary career spans governance, international development, technology for good, and human rights. From serving as Chairwoman of Concern Worldwide UK to her leadership roles at Oxford Policy Management, Moonshot CVE, and Apolitical, Bernadette has established herself as a global advocate for equity and sustainable progress.

Her expertise is advising governments, NGOs, and the private sector on implementing policies aligned with the Sustainable Development Goals (SDGs), focusing strongly on poverty alleviation and including marginalised groups. With a stellar academic background that includes an MBA, an MSc in Public Service Policy & Management, and a BA in History and Politics, Bernadette brings a rare blend of strategic vision and hands-on experience.

While Bernadette and I still haven't met for that long-promised drink, her generosity and willingness to contribute to this project without knowing me personally are a testament to the power of women pooling resources and supporting one another, and to her awesome character! Her ability to align diverse stakeholders and design ambitious yet actionable strategies ensured the Gender Action Plan resonated across industries, bridging the gap between vision and execution.

Transformative Collaboration

Brenda and Bernadette exemplify the transformative power of combining academic insight with operational expertise. By offering their time and skills pro bono, they eliminated the argument that financial constraints were a barrier to progress. Their work reinforced a fundamental truth: diversity, equity, and inclusion are not optional ideals but essential pillars of a thriving industry.

Their collaboration turned an abstract vision into a tangible, replicable framework that media organisations could adopt immediately. Together, they proved that bold leadership, deep expertise, and an unwavering commitment to justice can drive real change.

This partnership illustrates the power of collective action. Women's collective efforts, resource sharing, and refusal to accept the status quo can lay the groundwork for transformative advances. The Gender Action Plan is a testament to what's possible when passion meets purpose. Brenda and Bernadette's work will reverberate for years, fuelling the movement for a more inclusive media landscape.

Breaking Down the Excuses

One of the most persistent counterarguments we encountered was the myth of meritocracy. Critics claimed that prioritising diversity meant compromising on quality—a deeply flawed narrative that perpetuates exclusion and undermines progress.

Research continues to dismantle this misconception. Studies have shown that gender quotas can significantly enhance organisational performance. For example, research published in the *Journal of Leadership and Governance* highlights that quotas increase workplace diversity, which directly improves decision-making and fosters innovation. Another study analysing California's gender quota law observed that companies adopting quotas experienced a shift towards long-term strategic investments, including greater focus on research and development and organisational growth.

These findings affirm what we already know from experience: talent is everywhere, but opportunities are not. Opportunities don't appear magically—they must be created. Without quotas or deliberate structural change, the cycle of exclusion continues unabated.

Practical Solutions: The Three Pillars of Change

By outlining three straightforward pillars, the Gender Action Plan removed every possible excuse for inaction, proving that meaningful change is achievable without financial barriers:

Leaders Commit to Equal Representation: Leadership must set clear diversity metrics, integrate them into organisational strategies, and track progress regularly. This is less about cost and more about intent. Leadership sets the tone—if diversity is a priority at the top, it becomes a priority throughout the organisation.

Data-Driven Decision-Making: Data is a powerful tool for identifying gaps and measuring progress. By analysing playlists, airplay minutes, and audience demographics, stations can track their performance and hold themselves accountable. The tools to do this already exist; the only requirement is the will to use them.

Be Champions of Change: Cultural shifts require active participation. Leaders and staff must embody inclusive behaviours, fostering an environment where diversity isn't just a goal but a shared value. This involves more than policy; it's about cultivating a workplace culture that celebrates and promotes diverse perspectives.

By offering these solutions for free, we removed every possible excuse. The result? More organisations rose to the challenge, proving resource limitations were not an obstacle but a matter of attitude.

No More Excuses

The truth is that diversity is not just morally important; it is also necessary. Audiences expect it, advertisers reward it, and artists benefit from it. The route forward is clear. Excuses just hold us back; taking action moves us toward a more inclusive, creative, and successful profession. The question is not whether change is feasible, but whether those in power would choose to embrace it.

Despite these apparent benefits, resistance—yes, that word again, making its grand 457th appearance in this book (you're welcome)—persists. Some organisations have gracefully hopped aboard the change gravy train, while others are still clinging to outdated norms like a cat to a piece of string. And so, advocacy remains essential—not just to spark change but to keep it alive and well, like the plant you swore you'd water daily… but actually will this time.

The other great thing about The Gender Action Plan was that it showed what's possible when excuses are set aside. But the journey doesn't end with frameworks—it continues with accountability, persistence, and a commitment to leaving no voice unheard.

With every step forward—every playlist diversified, every barrier broken—we prove excuses are just that: excuses. Change is possible. The only question is whether those in power will embrace it.

Chapter 13

THE SOUND OF CHANGE

"Equality is not a gift to be granted—it is a right to be reclaimed. When one voice speaks up, it sparks change. When many voices rise together, it becomes a revolution that no system can silence."
– Linda Coogan Byrne.

For years, we've been told to wait—told that progress takes time and patience is a virtue. I'm not sure if I mentioned this earlier, but during my first meeting with the team from the Broadcasting Authority of Ireland (now called Coimisiún na Meán), they told me quite directly that I wasn't the first—and wouldn't be the last—to ask for change. They also mentioned that even remote changes would take at least five years.

But how much patience is enough when women and marginalised voices are still fighting for the right to be heard? Change doesn't happen by waiting—it happens by demanding, disrupting, and refusing to settle for less. From my perspective, we must continue to advocate for equal rights: the right to be heard, acknowledged, and to occupy the same spaces as men without facing doubts or criticisms about being "too emotional" or "too focused" on starting a family.

Women in the workplace—whether in music, media, or any male-dominated field—face a prejudice so ingrained that it rarely needs to be spoken aloud. Employers see a young woman with ambition and potential, and instead of thinking of a future leader, they think of a future maternity leave. Decision-makers quietly deny promotions, leave contracts unsigned, and redirect opportunities to male counterparts, whom they see as less of a "risk."

When men take an active role in parenting, they're praised for doing the bare minimum. A father wheels a buggy through a park, and suddenly, he's a hands-on dad. A man changes a nappy? Wow, how progressive! Meanwhile, mothers juggle work, childcare, and the crushing weight of societal demands, and no one blinks.

It's not just frustrating—it's insulting. Baked into that over-the-top celebration of fatherhood is an ugly truth: society still sees parenting as women's work. Society views a man's choice to engage in parenting as a bonus, an act of generosity. For women, there is no choice—only expectation. If a woman decides she doesn't want to have children at all? Well, then she's labelled cold, selfish, unnatural. A male-centric world limits women's purpose to motherhood or nothingness.

Motherhood vs. Music: The Industry's Double Standard

In the music industry, this bias takes on a sharper edge. Time and again, female artists are asked, 'How do you manage being a mother while touring?' The implication is clear: their artistry is secondary to their role as mothers. Male artists? They're never asked to justify their work-life balance because society has already decided their work comes first.

Have you ever heard a male artist asked during a press interview, 'How do you juggle fatherhood with being on the road?' Of course not—because men aren't expected to juggle anything. They're allowed to be artists first, no questions asked. Meanwhile, female musicians, no matter how successful, are almost always seen as mothers first and artists second.

Here's the thing—it's not just men asking these questions. Women in the media do it too. They should know better, yet they still fall into the trap of reinforcing the biases that have held us back for generations. These questions aren't harmless. They send a clear message—your role as a mother matters more than your role as an artist. This mindset prevents women from headlining, keeps them from festivals, and forces them to fight for the same recognition men receive automatically.

The Nina Simone Effect: A Woman's Genius Comes at a Cost

One of Nina Simone's most famous quotes about her artistry speaks to the raw, unfiltered truth of what it means to be an artist and a woman navigating the world:

"An artist's duty is to reflect the times in which we live."

What happens when the artist is also a mother? What happens when the world refuses to let her be both?

Nina Simone—one of the most revolutionary voices in music—gave everything to her art but, in doing so, faced relentless judgment for neglecting motherhood. Critics painted her as a complex woman, an unstable genius, and a lousy mother. Her daughter, Lisa Simone, has spoken openly about the struggles of growing up with a mother whose artistry and activism consumed her. People overlook the impossible choice Simone was compelled to make—one that male artists never had to make.

When men dedicate themselves fully to their craft, they are visionaries. It's seen as self-indulgent when women engage in this. When men put their art before their families, they are tortured geniuses. When women do the same, they are neglectful, unfit, and unnatural.

Sinéad O'Connor, Poly Styrene, and the Cost of Defiance

Many voices in the music industry have exemplified the unyielding resilience and strength of feminist defiance. If I were to highlight just three figures who truly embodied this—the fight, the rebellion, the raw, unshakable truth of standing against injustice—it would be Sinéad O'Connor, Poly Styrene, and Nina Simone.

Sinéad O'Connor stepped into a fire knowing she would be burnt, yet she did it anyway. It was who she was. Her willpower, refusal to give up, and unwavering courage in the face of injustice made her a trailblazer in every respect. She, like Poly Styrene and Nina Simone before her, faced continual criticism; nonetheless, it was their agony and tenacity that lay the framework for the conflicts we continue to fight in the music industry today.

Sinéad. She was something else. Always with a giant 'not two fucks given'. Decades before the world had the spine to acknowledge the Catholic Church's crimes, she tore up a picture of the Pope on live television—knowing the backlash that would come—and stood steadfast, often alone, speaking out on mental health, misogyny, and Ireland's culture of silence. They called her a troublemaker, a disgrace, a woman falling apart—not because she was wrong, but because she was right far too early. And for that, they crucified her. When I sent the data reports to Sinéad, she said 'same shit, different era'. She knew. She lived it.

Poly Styrene tore through the punk scene as a mixed-race, working-class woman fronting a band in 1970s Britain. She famously defied the notion that 'little girls should be seen and not heard,' rejecting the status quo with a battle cry that became punk legend. Her lyrics ripped apart capitalism, sexism, and racism. She was dismissed as 'too much,' 'unstable,' and 'unmarketable.' But she didn't care. She was punk through and through.

And yet, after their deaths, the same industry that shunned them claimed them as icons.

The Revolution Continues

This manifesto is more than simply a reflection on what has been accomplished; it is also a road map for what is yet to come. The fight for equality in the music industry has not magically ended, but the route forward is clear. Every voice raised, every barrier broken, and every step taken together brings us closer to a society in which no one is silenced and everyone is recognised.

I am just one more person standing in front of the establishment, asking them: Why Not Her?

Now is our time. Let us keep going.

Sinéad. Poly. Nina. Three women from three different countries, in distinct eras, fighting the same damn battle. They were brilliant. They were brave. They were demonised for it. And now, it's on us. Because their stories are our stories, their struggles—the punishment they endured for being too loud, too opinionated, and too unwilling to conform—are still happening today.

If these women taught us anything, it's that we cannot afford to stop, shrink, or apologise. Their voices were the first notes in a symphony of change—it's up to us to carry the melody forward, louder and more unapologetically than ever before.

I don't know where you come from. As for me?

I come from a lineage of women who understood that survival isn't a given—it's a battle, a skill forged out of necessity. These were women who carried the weight of unspeakable things in their bones, and who swallowed silence like it was nourishment because there was no other choice. But silence was their inheritance—not ours. It will not be passed down like an heirloom, wrapped in whispered warnings.

"Courage calls to courage everywhere." – *Millicent Fawcett*.

And in that courage, we are gifted a choice.

If we dare to break the cycle, name the unnameable, and speak even when our voices tremble, we can end the silence.

We are not here to inherit their suffering. We are here to honour their fight—to continue what they began, or to pay respect to whatever fear prevented them from finishing. We will give voice to those who cannot speak for themselves, tearing down the barriers they could only crack.

I leave you with this: never underestimate the power of a single voice. When it joins with others, it becomes unstoppable. As Nina Simone sang in *Revolution*, "We're in the middle of a revolution, 'cause I see the face of things to come." Close your eyes and picture it—the face of things to come. It's your face. It's the face of your neighbour. It's the face of a girl in Tehran, a boy in Lagos, a woman in Gaza, a nonbinary artist in São Paulo, a grandmother in Dublin who dreams of witnessing change in her lifetime, a daughter in New York, a wife in Ukraine, and a son in London. It's every shade, every wrinkle of wisdom, every spark of defiance, every tear wiped away as we walk, together, toward a better day.

The faces of those yet to come are the faces we fight for—faces full of potential, resilience, and the brilliance of unspoken dreams. Together, we're not just singing a song or writing a story; we are orchestrating a movement—a symphony of voices rising in unison. Let those faces remind you that change doesn't come from waiting—it comes from daring to demand more and believing, against all odds, that we are capable of building something better.

And when the music swells and your voice joins the chorus, remember: you are not alone. You are part of the revolution, shaping the face of what's to come. Preparing the songs yet to be sung. Let us make sure it's a song that echoes justice, equality, and the courage to fight for both.

The End.

EPILOGUE

LOOKING FORWARD: THE MOVEMENT CONTINUES & AN ACTIVIST'S TOOLKIT FOR CHANGE

This manifesto is more than a reflection of the past six years—it is a blueprint for the road ahead. If you are ready to fight for gender and racial equality, I hope this inspires you to take action because the world desperately needs voices like ours.

As we look forward, it's clear that the fight for equity and inclusion isn't over. But it's also clear that change is possible—with the right tools, persistence, and collective effort. Below is a roadmap to guide the work that still lies ahead.

1. Expanding Advocacy

- **Global Partnerships:** Forge alliances with international feminist organisations to share resources, amplify voices, and coordinate efforts across borders.

- **Diversifying Reports**: Broaden the scope of disparity reports to include music, media, and other creative industries like film, literature, and technology.

- **Public Awareness Campaigns**: Launch campaigns highlighting gender disparities, using compelling narratives and data to educate the public and inspire action.

- **Youth Engagement:** Develop programmes and initiatives to involve younger generations and empower them to take leadership roles in Advocacy.

2. Policy Engagement

- **Legislative Collabouration:** Work closely with policymakers to draft, implement, and refine laws to achieve gender balance in all public-facing industries.

- **Incentivising Change:** Advocate for grants, tax incentives, and funding opportunities to support underrepresented creators and organisations prioritising diversity.

- **Accountability Mechanisms**: Push for establishing independent bodies to monitor and enforce compliance with gender and diversity standards.

- **Policy Education**: Conduct training sessions and provide resources to policymakers, helping them understand the systemic barriers and the steps needed to dismantle them.

3. Community Building

- **Workshops and Panels**: Organise regular events that unite activists, artists, and advocates to share insights, strategies, and experiences.

- **Safe Spaces:** Create platforms where marginalised voices can be heard without fear of backlash, fostering an environment of trust and collaboration.

- **Networking Opportunities:** Facilitate connections between like-minded individuals and organisations to strengthen the movement's impact.

- **Digital Communities**: Build and nurture online communities through forums, social media groups, and webinars to maintain momentum and global reach.

4. Ongoing Accountability

- **Annual Reporting**: Continue publishing detailed yearly reports that track progress, highlight successes, and identify improvement areas.

- **Celebrating Wins**: Showcase success stories to inspire others and demonstrate that persistence and collective effort make change possible.

- **Transparent Communication**: Maintain open lines of communication with stakeholders, ensuring they are informed and involved in the movement's initiatives.

- **Evaluation Frameworks**: Develop and implement tools to assess the effectiveness of campaigns and policies, using the findings to guide future strategies.

An Activist's Toolkit for Change

I couldn't leave the end of the book without offering you some form of a toolkit to get you started! Activism is both a calling and a battlefield, a place where hope and exhaustion coexist, victories are fleeting, and backlash is inevitable. This is not just a checklist—it's a guide to surviving and sustaining your fire while navigating the complexities of Advocacy.

This toolkit is designed to empower individuals and organisations to drive meaningful change, but more importantly, it's here to help you *stay the course*. Because activism isn't just about starting a movement—it's about *enduring* one.

1. How to Start a Movement (Without Burning Out)

- **Identify the issue you're passionate about.** It's not just something that makes you angry in passing but a cause you'd be willing to fight for even when you're exhausted, demoralised, and questioning your impact.
- **Build a team of like-minded individuals.** No one sustains a movement alone. Find those who share your vision but bring different strengths—organisers, designers, researchers, speakers, and strategists.
- **Leverage social media—but don't let it consume you.** Social media is a double-edged sword. It can amplify your message but become an echo chamber where performative activism drowns tangible action. Use it wisely, but never mistake virality for real-world change.

Reality Check:

Movements are not built overnight. They take time, persistence, and, often, a lot of behind-the-scenes, thankless work. If you're not prepared for slow, frustrating progress, you will burn out before you make an impact.

2. Using Data for Advocacy: The Power of Truth

- **Collect and analyse relevant data to uncover systemic issues.** Numbers can be manipulated, but when used effectively, they can expose patterns of discrimination and injustice that can't be ignored.
- **Present findings in transparent, visual formats.** Decision-makers respond to facts, but *people* react to stories. Use both.
- **Share reports with stakeholders to spark conversations.** The truth is only as powerful as the people who hear it. Get it before policymakers, journalists, and community leaders who can help enact change.

When I first started compiling gender disparity data reports, the pushback was immediate. Radio stations called the data "inaccurate," and industry leaders dismissed it as a "coincidence." But once the evidence was out there—undeniable and irrefutable—change began. Not all at once, not everywhere, but the cracks in the old systems started to show. Be consistent and find suitable allies.

Reality Check:

Data alone won't change the world—*action* does. Be ready for institutions to ignore, discredit, or twist your findings to maintain the status quo. Stay persistent. The truth *will* cut through.

3. Effective Messaging: The Art of Making People Care

- **Craft a compelling mission statement.** If you can't sum up your movement's goal in one sentence, you're not ready to rally people behind it.
- **Use storytelling to humanise your cause.** People don't just rally behind statistics—they rally behind *stories*. A single, personal testimony can often move hearts more than a 50-page report. Having both is ideal.
- **Tailor messages for different audiences.** What moves the general public may not sway policymakers, and what speaks to journalists may not reach grassroots organisers. Adapt without compromising your integrity.

Reality Check:

Your message will be distorted, misrepresented, taken out of context, or used against you. Be prepared for criticism and learn to distinguish between *constructive feedback* and *bad-faith attacks*. A very thick neck will be required. It is not for the faint-hearted.

4. Engaging Policymakers: Navigating the Bureaucratic Beast

- **Research existing policies and identify gaps.** Know the laws that govern your issue inside and out. The more informed you are, the harder it will be to dismiss you.
- **Schedule meetings with representatives and present actionable solutions.** Policy change doesn't happen through outrage alone. When you approach those in power, have clear, implementable solutions.

- **Follow up consistently to ensure progress.** Politicians move at a glacial pace—until there's public pressure. Be the pressure.

Reality Check:

Legislation is not a magic fix. Laws can be passed and not enforced, and policies can be changed and ignored. The real work begins *after* the headline-grabbing victory.

5. Community Building: No One Fights Alone

- **Organise events that foster collaboration and dialogue.** Activism thrives on connection. Create spaces where people can gather, share ideas, and build solidarity.
- **Highlight the contributions of diverse voices within your movement.** If your activism only centres on *you*, it's not a movement—it's a brand. Make space for others, especially those most impacted by the injustice you're fighting.
- **Encourage mutual support and solidarity.** The fight is long. Take care of each other.

In every campaign I've worked on, the moments that mattered most weren't the big wins—they were the quiet acts of solidarity, the late-night phone calls between activists drowning in threats, and the emails and messages of support when the backlash became unbearable. Movements survive because people *hold each other up*.

Reality Check:

You will be disappointed. You will lose people along the way. It will hurt. Not everyone will stay when the fight gets hard. But the ones who do? They are worth everything.

6. Maintaining Resilience: Surviving the Fight

- **Prioritise mental health and self-care.** Burnout doesn't make you a better activist. Rest is not a betrayal of the cause—it is what allows you to keep going.
- **Celebrate milestones and small victories.** Not every win will be monumental. But progress, no matter how small, is still progress.
- **Build a support network of allies and collaborators.** You need people who will remind you why you started when you feel like giving up.

Reality Check:

You will face opposition, be threatened, be exhausted, heartbroken, and angry. The system is designed to wear you down. *Don't let it.*

AFTERWORD
THE FIRE THAT KEEPS US MOVING

A s Angela Davis reminds us, 'I am no longer accepting what I cannot alter. I'm changing the things I can't accept.' These words define our mission. This fight is not about achieving perfection; it's about driving progress. Standing still is not an option in a world that urgently demands action.

We are fighting for progress, not perfection. Because standing stagnant is surrendering, and those who dare to dream of a better future have never had that option. From Ida B. Wells, who bravely exposed injustice with her pen, to Emmeline Pankhurst, who reminded us, "We are here, not because we are lawbreakers, but in our efforts to become lawmakers."

If the feminists and suffragettes of the past had silenced their voices or lowered their hands, we wouldn't stand where we are today. They faced violence, ridicule, and unimaginable hardships so we could vote, work, love, and live freely. They climbed, risked, and sacrificed so we could rise higher.

Audre Lorde, the voice of many silent, once said, "When we speak, we are scared our words will not be heard or welcomed. But even when we remain silent, we are terrified. So it's better to speak."

We become stronger together, not just as feminists but as a global resistance movement. We challenge systems, break silences, and alter narratives. We are the seeds of their hopes, the echo of their chants, and the architects of a future in which every voice and narrative is valued.

So, if they try to silence you, let your voice rise louder. If they attempt to extinguish your fire, let it blaze bolder. Or as my Nana used to always say, *go on out and stir that shit*. This movement thrives because of people like you—unwavering, unyielding, and unstoppable.

REFERENCES AND FURTHER READING

Here's a list of sources, reports, and books that have informed and inspired this work and will help those who want to dig deeper into the gender and racial disparities in the music industry and beyond. Big love to everyone who worked on these important studies, reports and books.

Key Reports & Studies

- **Why Not Her? Gender & Racial Disparity Data Reports** – Gender Disparity Data Reports on Irish and UK Radio https://whynother.eu/data-reports
- **Progressing Gender Representation in UK Dance Music** – Commissioned by The Jaguar Foundation with support from Sony Music UK's Social Justice Fund, this report provides an in-depth analysis of gender balance within the UK dance music scene and offers recommendations for improvement. https://www.thejaguarfoundation.net/report
- **Inclusion in the Recording Studio?** – Conducted by the Annenberg Inclusion Initiative, this study examines the representation of women in various roles within the music

industry, highlighting the underrepresentation of women producers. annenberg.usc.edu

- **Musicians' Census Report** – Published by the Musicians' Union, this report reveals that over half of women in music have experienced gender discrimination and highlights the underrepresentation of women in technical roles such as sound engineering and production. https://musiciansunion.org.uk/news/musicians-census-finds-over-half-of-women-in-music-have-experienced-gender-discrimination

- **Be the Change: Gender Equity in Music** – A report by MIDiA Research that takes an intersectional approach to mapping the impacts of overlapping forms of discrimination in the music industry. midiaresearch.com

- **The Annenberg Inclusion Initiative: Music Industry Reports** – US-based data on gender representation in music https://annenberg.usc.edu/news/research-and-impact/women-music-hold-gains-have-more-room-grow

- **Fix the Mix Report (2023)** – A deep dive into gender disparities in audio production and engineering https://w1.mtsu.edu/media/fix.pdf

- **Gender Balance in Lineups** – By Vick Bain https://vbain.co.uk/how-to-achieve-gender-balance-in-line-ups/

- **Keychange manifesto** – https://www.keychange.eu/about-us/news-feed-articles/rewind-and-fast-forward-keychange-announces-impact-evaluation-report-2018-2023-and-unveils-keychange-manifesto-20

- **The USC Inclusion in the Recording Studio** – Gender & Race/Ethnicity of Artists, Songwriters & Producers across 1,300 Popular Songs from 2012 to 2024 - https://assets.uscannenberg.org/docs/aii-inclusion-recording-studio-2025-01-29-2.pdf

BOOKS & ARTICLES

- **She Bop**: *The Definitive History of Women in Popular Music* – Lucy O'Brien
- **Women Make Noise**: *Girl Bands from Motown to Modern* – Julia Downes
- **Sounds Like A Revolution** – Nadine Hubbs
- **The Problem with Muzak**: *A Feminist History of the Music Industry* – Hannah McGregor
- **Women & Power**: *A Manifesto* - Mary Beard
- **Why Feminism Matters in the Music Industry** – Ruth Pearce
- **The Power of Women in Music** – Jennifer Lucy Allan
- **Girls to the Front**: *The True Story of the Riot Grrrl Revolution* – Sara Marcus
- **Misogyny, Music & the Industry** – Vick Bain
- **Invisible Women**: *Exposing Data Bias in a World Designed for Men* – Caroline Criado-Perez
- **Hood Feminism**: *Notes from the Women That a Movement Forgot* – Mikki Kendall

- ***Mediocre:** The Dangerous Legacy of White Male America -* – Ijeoma Oluo
- ***The Seven Necessary Sins for Women and Girls*** – Mona Eltahawy
- ***Femina***: A New History of the Middle Ages, Through the Women Written Out of It - Janina Ramirez

100 WOMEN IN MUSIC YOU SHOULD KNOW (UK & IRELAND)

Over the past two years, a wave of incredible women has been reshaping the music landscape across the UK and Ireland, pushing boundaries in rock, pop, folk, electronic, jazz, classical, and beyond. They may not always dominate the front of every major festival bill or land on every heavily rotated radio playlist, but that doesn't mean they aren't **smashing glass ceilings, carving out space, and leading the charge for a more diverse, innovative, and authentic music industry.** Each of these artists is redefining what success looks like—on their own terms.

In the UK, artists like **Arlo Parks, Nova Twins, Little Simz, Self Esteem, Raye, Holly Humberstone, Jorja Smith, Mahalia, Georgia, Sinead Harnett, Celeste, Låpsley, Jessie Ware, FKA twigs, Shygirl, Alewya, ENNY, Greentea Peng, Becky Hill, FLO, Baby Queen, Beabadoobee, Biig Piig, Nia Archives, Joy Crookes, Yazmin Lacey, The Last Dinner Party, Miraa May, Rachel Chinouriri, Anna Meredith, Kelly Lee Owens, Poppy Ajudha, Eliza Shaddad, Bessie Turner, Saint Clair, Nadine Shah, Charlotte OC, Imogen Heap, The Big Moon, Anna Calvi, Bat for Lashes, Lucinda Chua, Rebecca Ferguson, Olivia Dean, Sophie**

Ellis-Bextor, Ayanna Witter-Johnson, and Nilüfer Yanya are all making waves. Women in rock are breaking new ground, too, with **Wolf Alice, Dream Wife, and Pale Waves** leading the charge.

Meanwhile, Ireland has seen a surge in powerful voices across multiple genres. **CMAT, Denise Chaila, Sinead White, RuthAnne, Tolü Makay, Roisin Murphy, Ailbhe Reddy, Soulé, Sorcha Richardson, Erica Cody, Wallis Bird, Shiv, Elaine Mai, Jess Kav, Kehli, Róisín O, Fia Moon, Krea, Lisa Hannigan, LYRA, Aby Coulibaly, Emma Langford, Síomha, Eve Belle, Saint Sister, Wyvern Lingo, Maria Kelly, Loah, Pillow Queens, Aoife Nessa Frances, Maria Doyle Kennedy, Brigid Mae Power, Nnic, Havvk, Pauline Scanlon, Farah Elle, Susan O'Neill, Eleanor McEvoy, Lilla Vargen, Sophie Doyle Ryder, Imelda May, Rachael Lavelle, Sharon Shannon, Áine Tyrrell, Karan Casey, Lisa Canny, Winnie Ama, and Lorraine Nash** continue to bring fresh perspectives and sounds to the forefront.

These are just some of the voices shaping the industry today, and you can listen to them all in this **curated playlist here:**

https://open.spotify.com/playlist/78B81evzLrmrHTACkUpaUT?si=148e3a4680a043c9 .

Go out and seek more! Be curious, explore beyond the mainstream, and discover the incredible talent that's waiting to be heard. Most importantly, be part of the solution to the question, **Why Not Her?**

ABOUT THE COVER ARTWORK

The cover for Why Not Her? was designed by Paul Holbrook-Phillips of True Spilt Milk, an award-winning designer and illustrator known for his intricate and colourful artwork. Paul's aesthetic, shaped by his deep roots in the music scene, captures the spirit of this manifesto with striking symbolism and bold design.

The Bird—A Crow — A symbol of freedom and defiance. With the microphone in its grasp, the bird embodies the act of women seizing the mic—taking back their voices and demanding to be heard. It flies beyond reach, a powerful metaphor for autonomy and the refusal to be silenced. In Celtic mythology, the crow is deeply linked to feminine power, transformation, and prophecy, often associated with the Morrígan, the warrior goddess who presides over fate, sovereignty, and the shifting tides of battle. Here, the crow channels that ancient energy—a force of reckoning, watching over change, ensuring that truth and justice are spoken into being. Like the Morrígan's presence on the battlefield, this crow reminds us that words hold power, and when wielded with intent, they can reshape the world.

The Microphone and Cord—Paul envisioned the microphone cord intertwining with the letters of the title, connecting voice with message, art with activism. The flowing line suggests movement, dialogue, and the threads of conversation that drive change.

The Bold Typography—The title Why Not Her? is rendered in bold, oversized type because the question it poses should be as loud and unapologetic as the fight for equity itself.

The Colours and Background — The textured blue background, reminiscent of an open sky, evokes freedom and possibility. Initially, Paul considered a palette of blue and pink—a subtle nod to traditional gender hues—but chose instead to let the blue sky stand alone, a reflection on inclusivity beyond gender binaries.

Paul's design is more than a cover—it's a statement, a conversation, and a call to action.

ABOUT THE AUTHOR

Linda Coogan Byrne is a globally recognised music publicist, writer, artist, journalist, and entertainment consultant with over two decades of experience in the music and media industries. As CEO of Good Seed PR, she has led groundbreaking campaigns for internationally acclaimed artists and emerging talent across multiple genres. Renowned for her expertise in artist development, branding, and media strategy, Linda has established herself as one of the most trusted voices in music PR, known for delivering meaningful impact and cultural change.

Beyond PR, Linda is a driving force for diversity, equity, and inclusion in the music industry. As CEO of Why Not Her?, she has spearheaded efforts to dismantle systemic biases in Irish and UK radio, championing gender and racial parity. Her pioneering Gender & Racial Disparity Data Reports have reached millions of people, igniting global conversations and catalysing policy changes. The #WhyNotHer movement, born from her research, has become a rallying call for justice in media representation.

A respected writer and thought leader, Linda's work has been featured in The Guardian, The Times, The Telegraph, The Examiner, Daily Mail, Metro, BBC, RTE, and IQ Magazine. She has been recognised among Ireland's Top 100 Most Influential Women (2021) and Top 20 (2024) and was a Campaigner of the Year nominee at the 2023 Music Week Awards before being inducted into the Music Week Hall of Honour (2024).

An in-demand public speaker, Linda has delivered talks and guest lectures at universities across Ireland and the UK, as well as major industry events, including Hotpress MixSix, OutPut, FFWD London, BBC Big Weekend, Metropolis, and MUTEK Barcelona. Through her advocacy, research, and voice, she continues to challenge the status quo, shaping the future of music and media for generations to come.

SOURCES & ATTRIBUTIONS

The following quotes appear in *Why Not Her? A Manifesto For Culture Change* and are credited to their original sources, listed in chronological order by chapter:

Chapter 1: Amplifying Voices – Where the Journey Begins

- *"Ní Saoirse go Saoirse na mBan: There is no freedom until the freedom of women."*
  Source: Old Irish Proverb.

Chapter 2: Beyond the Stage – Dismantling Systemic Inequalities

- *"The systemic change we need isn't about tearing anyone down—it's about building everyone up."*
  Source: Roxane Gay, *Bad Feminist* (2014).

Chapter 3: The Power of Data

- *"Data is a precious thing and will last longer than the systems themselves."*
  Source: Tim Berners-Lee, *Weaving the Web* (1999).

Chapter 4: Turning Data Into Action

- *"Data has the power to expose inequality and drive accountability. But it is not enough to see the numbers—we must act to transform them into justice."*
  Source: Mary Robinson, Speech at the UN on Gender Equity (2016).

Chapter 5: The Boundless Potential of Women

- *"I demand the independence of woman, her right to support herself; to live for herself; to love whomever she pleases, or as many as she pleases."*
  Source: Emma Goldman, *Anarchism and Other Essays* (1910).

Chapter 6: The Light Switch Moment

- *"When a man gives his opinion, he's a man. When a woman gives her opinion, she's a bitch."*
  Source: Bette Davis.

Chapter 7: Diving Into the Data

- *"Data is not just about numbers; it's about the lives and realities they represent. The real power lies in what we do with it."*
  Source: Catherine D'Ignazio, *Data Feminism* (2020).

Chapter 8: Driving Change – The People and the Proof

- *"Never doubt that a small group of thoughtful, committed citizens can change the world. Indeed, it is the only thing that ever has."*
  Source: Margaret Mead.

Chapter 9: Follow the Money and Amplify Your Influence

- *"Whoever controls the media, the images, controls the culture."*
  Source: Allen Ginsberg.

Chapter 10: Why Not Her? Turning Visibility into Victory

- *"The Master's Tools Will Never Dismantle the Master's House."*
  Source: Audre Lorde.

Chapter 13: The Sound of Change

- *"An artist's duty is to reflect the times in which we live."*
  Source: Nina Simone, *Jet Magazine Interview* (1968).

- *"Same shit, different era."*
  Source: Sinéad O'Connor, originally posted on Twitter.

www.ingramcontent.com/pod-product-compliance
Lightning Source LLC
Chambersburg PA
CBHW051600010526
44118CB00023B/2766